THE BRIDGE

THE BRIDGE

NATHAN PEACOCK

COPYRIGHT

REVIEWS

If you are curious about God, if you question His existence, or if you are a Christ follower–this book will help guide you to a better understanding of our Creator God. Nathan does an excellent job of sharing his personal, professional, and spiritual journey. You will experience every human emotion and share some amazing moments as you come to know this not so "ordinary guy."

Wyatt Matthews

DEDICATION

For my family–my wife, Cheryl, and my children, Jennifer, Eric, and Anne. Thank you for your patience while I learned to be a husband and father.

A special thank you to my eldest daughter, Jennifer, who spent countless hours pulling facts out of my head to help me compile the early manuscripts, which I refer to as my crayon editions, and transform them into readable text. Thanks Pep.

Thank you, God, for using the apparition to point me toward You in all things, making an impression on my life in such a hopeful, beneficial way.

AUTHOR'S BIO

I never really wanted to write this book for two reasons. The first was the supernatural event that I experienced as a young adult radically changed who I was, but I was afraid to share it for fear of what others would think. The second, I had to live for the next forty years before I realized why the supernatural event was part of my life in the first place. Looking back, I might not have been able to bear the emotional overload of dealing with the continuous tragedy working as a firefighter- paramedic, and witnessing some of the most horrific conditions imaginable, without the hope from my life-event so many years before. Working thirty-five years at some of the busiest firehouses in a large metropolitan city, I came to realize that my entire life had been far from normal. My coworkers would tell me that someone needs to write this stuff down; no one would ever believe it. My family would echo my coworkers' requests for me to pick up a pen, so I finally did. It took two years to produce a rough manuscript, not because I am so slow, which I can be, but because pulling up these stories deeply embedded in my brain meant reliving them. As I wrote the book, I periodically, inadvertently, shifted my writing style to present tense, as I found myself experiencing the events and emotions all over again. Therapy came in the retelling, as finally processing the suppressed memories brought peace. Now retired, I live in a modest house in the burbs with my wife and a yellow lab named Cooper. The transition from my former life is different--surreal, as if I now live in some kind of alternate reality. Sometimes when I am sleeping, I will hear the wailing of nighttime first-responder sirens responding to emergency calls. I pull my blanket up and go back to sleep.

CONTENTS

INTRODUCTION

Nothing about the manifestation of the apparition four decades ago was a naturally occurring phenomenon in our world–inexplicable, it danced on the edge of truth and reality. The appearance was permanently seared in my mind, unchanging, as clear today as when I experienced it forty years ago. Still the mystery evokes endless emotion. I found myself pondering the unending questions–with only some being answered through deep thought and time. Others still lingered, like the questions one has while staring at the stars, unable to grasp the vastness of the endless canopy above.

To begin to answer any of the questions, I realized there must be a shift in the type of analysis of the apparition from a physical, scientific exploration to a metaphysical, subjective interpretation detached from scientific analysis.

Why? Because science can be inadequate when addressing the supernatural. Science falls short with answers to supernatural questions. Science can describe what a dog is, for example, through thorough physiological analysis of the mammal. Scientific analysis cannot answer the question of why some dogs will stay with their master after the master has broken a leg and is trapped in the woods, lost and starving. Dogs will endure hunger, remain with the master, or in some cases, will even search for help. Dogs have been known to travel for hundreds of miles to be reunited with their masters. What in a dog makes some of them appear so loyal? Science has insufficient answers. We don't know either; we just know it happens, and it's real.

The following is my attempt to answer questions that others may have pondered for centuries, as I learned them through my life as a firefighter, paramedic, Bible teacher, and Christ follower. The same question remains today as when I initially observed the apparition: *Why did it occur? Why the appearance? And equally as valid, why me? Why did I see the apparition and maybe not others? Most importantly, what long-term effect did the sighting have on the recipient?* A thorough analysis may yield answers to these questions. This book is a presentation of my attempt to analyze and answer these questions and more. Let's start with me, an ordinary guy.

CHAPTER 1

An Ordinary Guy

It was hot. It always seemed hot where I grew up. My oldest brother took a raw egg outside one sweltering afternoon in an attempt to fry it on the sidewalk. This egg didn't cook all the way through, but I have certainly seen people eat eggs cooked much less than his egg.

In the front window of our house hung a swamp cooler to give some relief from the unbearable heat. A swamp cooler is really nothing more than a square, metal enclosure with wet straw lining the inside. A fan inside the structure blows damp, ninety-degree air into the house on one-hundred-degree days. The damp air deposits a light green layer of mildew on everything in the house, especially in the closet.

On hot days, which was all of them except two weeks in the winter, I would run around barefoot most of the day–except on Sunday, when I had to put on my shoes to go to Sunday school and church. Dad would clean our mildewed shoes–shining them with shoe polish.

My bare feet were tough as nails–tough enough to run across rough ground without a thought. The only surface that could best my feet was an asphalt roadway in mid- afternoon, heat waves radiating from the black-top surface. It would get so hot that cars passing by would make a sound like tires rolling over sticky, hot, melted, black tar. The hotter the day, the softer the roadway. No place for bare feet.

My wardrobe ensemble was tailor-made for the typically hot weather. Outside kids, growing up in the 1950s, donned a standard outfit: bluejeans, with double-thick material sewn in at the knees so the denim only ripped above and below the vulcanized patch; jean cuffs hiked halfway up the calves for extra cooling (and to keep them from dragging the ground and creating more holes than the ones lining the knee patches); horizontal-striped t-shirt; and a baseball cap–worn so as to fold my ears down. Bare feet rounded out the look.

My dad worked in the oil field. Lucky for me and my brothers, dad used his skills welding oil-field pipe together to build us a swing set. This swing set was great, bigger than any you could buy. The chains supporting the wooden swing seats were always rusty, so when I would swing, the inside of my sweaty fingers would get coated in a rusty, brown film that was easily wiped away on my jeans. Since the chains were so long, it was easy to get up some speed and swing really high. Occasionally, too high. Slipping off the seat at high altitude is known to knock your breath out when crashing to the ground. Unable to breathe, much less cry, all of my four brothers would crowd around my fallen, silent, seemingly lifeless body while I gasped for air like a freshly caught catfish lying on a pickup truck tailgate.

After what seemed an eternity, my breath would return. Blaming the mishap on whoever or whatever made me fall out of the swing was standard protocol as it was never my fault.

Time spent in the swings, while breathing normally, would typically be spent peeling and eating fresh oranges and grapefruits that grew in the yard.

Dad also made a rope swing for us. He hung it from a big tree in the yard and tied a rolled up blanket on the rope for the seat. We swung on it a few times before Mom realized that Dad had tied one of her good blankets to the rope. Too late now. She didn't want it returned filthy. It didn't matter. Unless it was a family heirloom there was no need for a blanket in the house. It was too hot at night to even tolerate a sheet.

We would climb on top of our rabbit cage, rope swing in hand, to launch ourselves for maximum speed and altitude on the rope swing. We called the rope swing a "paddydad." Sometimes we would give rabbits a ride on the paddydad, holding them under our arms and swinging together. I'm sure they enjoyed it as much as we did. I took my rabbit, named Big Mama, to first grade at school for show and tell. Big Mama won a blue ribbon in the contest for being the biggest rabbit anyone had ever seen. She earned her name. She also earned the Mama portion of her name. She would pop out more baby rabbits than any rabbit I've ever seen. They multiplied like, uh, rabbits.

We had about two weeks of winter every year. Just enough time to pull out the one long-sleeved flannel shirt that I and each of my brothers owned. If I didn't like my flannel shirt, I could look at the flannel my older brother was wearing and know that next year it was mine. The winter wardrobe, the flannel shirt, would have mildew green shoulders and matching collar from hanging too long in the closet regardless of what color the shirt was. Inheriting an actual green flannel for next year's winter was always a plus since it camouflaged the mildew.

Our clothes were dirty, no, filthy, most of the time from playing outside all day. We never went inside the house. Too much mildew. From outward appearance, an observer would think we were a poor family. From my perspective, I didn't know what the word "poor" meant. If poor means having a roof over our heads and enough to eat, then yes, I guess we were poor. I never felt poor, running around outside all summer with watermelon juice and seeds stuck to the front of my mildewed, sweaty, dirty t-shirt, swing-set-chain rust all over my blue jeans and hands, and rabbit fur stuck to my sweaty underarms from swinging on the paddydad with Big Mama. If this is poor, there are worse things.

My four brothers and I liked to gather horned toads—we called them horny toads. We would stow them in large metal buckets to see how many we could catch. We played with them and were proud that we could catch as many as we did. Fifty horny toads in one bucket were not uncommon numbers. One night we accidentally left a bucket of horny toads inside the house. After going to bed, some of the horny toads escaped the bucket. My father got up in the middle of the night to use the restroom. He typically wore an undershirt and boxer shorts to bed. He didn't own a pair of slippers, or if he did, he never wore them. Probably mildewed. Crawling out of bed in pitch darkness, he trudged off barefoot toward the bathroom. No sound nor light in the house. Moving stealthily down the hall, trying to be quiet, he stepped on one of the fugitive horny toads. Horny toads get their name because of the sharp, needle-like horns on their body from head to toe. Once the horns penetrated the bottom of my father's foot, his voice pierced the silence in a loud, interrogatory fashion. He used a lot of words that I wasn't familiar with at the time, but we all understood the gist of what he declared at the top of his lungs.

My father, born in the 1920s, came of age during the Great Depression. He had two brothers and two sisters, all raised by a widowed mother. His father, my grandfather, burned to death when my father was ten years old. My grandfather had been a painter, decorator, and a part time musician. Coming home from a painting job, his clothes covered in paint thinner, he caught fire. His burns were so severe that he laid in bed for a year before succumbing to his injuries. These were no doubt hard times for my father, a young man at the tender age of ten years old. Having to help raise siblings and help his mother caused my father to become a caregiver early on in life. He was a middle child like me; two older siblings, two younger. Whichever sibling could earn money to help the family was compelled to do so. Harsh living conditions, coupled with the necessity to protect and care for his mother and siblings at such a young age, could either destroy his spirit or build mental toughness. He became mentally tough. Living in a large city during the Depression years forced him and his brothers to convey a tough appearance and identity to ward off the possibility of becoming a potential target of violent conflict. In tough neighborhoods the young men would adopt a certain gait, or style of walking that conveyed their potential for extreme violence. My father and his brothers even went so far as not to use their given names but were known as Butch, Slug, and Max, three characters not to mess with unless willing to pay a hefty price.

During the Great Depression, President Franklin Roosevelt created the Civilian Conservation Corp, or the CCC camps as it came to be known, to give young men jobs building roads, state parks, and other construction projects. My father went to work in the CCC camps. He was able to earn one dollar per day, which helped keep the family fed.

After the attack on Pearl Harbor in December 1941, my nineteen-year-old father rode a freight train with other men to the enlistment office and signed up to be an Army soldier. He spent the duration of the war in combat in Europe, fighting in major battles, including the Battle of the Bulge and the Normandy Invasion on D-Day. Returning home, he married my mother. He often told me that every day of his life after his years in combat was a piece of cake. Nothing in his life after the war came close to the tragedy and hardship of experiencing war.

My mother was raised in a different world than my father. He was raised in the big city; whereas, she was raised on a farm. The only similarities are they both had four siblings and they were both middle children. My mother's siblings were all girls. She was also an identical twin to one of her older siblings, which created an interesting dating experience when they were older. On double dates they would switch places with each other mid date–their dates unaware.

Her father, my grandfather, was an ivy-league professor at a university on the East Coast before my mother was born; however, he always wanted to farm. Moving to Arkansas, he met my grandmother, married, and became a cotton farmer. He loved to plow with mules. Even with the advent of the tractor, he continued to plow with mules. Makes one wonder whether he or the mules were more stubborn. He was a strong Christian man who used to spend time in the barn milking cows and singing spiritual songs. My mother, the obvious favorite of her father, a "daddy's girl," spent many hours with her father. My mother's father died young, and my mother, leaving the hardship of the farm, left with her twin to earn their living in the city. They both found jobs and moved into rooms at the YWCA where they lived until marriage.

The only one as tough as my father was my mother. My father married a woman with whom he could contend. If there were ever a Romeo and Juliet story it was my parents' story. They battled at times but had an undying love for each other that was the stabilizing glue in their relationship. It was more than just love for each other that held them together: commitment, respect, and the inner knowledge that they were both pulling the cart of life in the same direction, instead of being adversarial. They both wanted the same things out of life, and they knew those things would only materialize by staying together as one. Their plan worked. Growing up with my parents, my four brothers and I never entertained the thought that they might split up; it would have been unheard of with these two. They were bound together, whether in chaos or order, as they faced the world as one.

I grew up attending a Baptist church. As a little boy my parents would take us to church just about every Sunday. We would go to Sunday School, and then attend church with our parents. The goal for our parents, and it seemed most parents in a Baptist church in the 1950s, was to have all their children publicly profess Christ as their personal Lord and Savior and declare the fact to the world through public baptism. Our new-found Christianity would be official; the church would issue a certificate of baptism.

We moved from a small rural town to a big city when I was about eight years old. Living in a big city meant going to a different church. We shopped around for a different Baptist church to attend and settled on the Second Baptist Church. I don't know how or why it was named Second Baptist, there were probably a hundred Baptist churches in that city. Once my parents decided where we would go to church, the next step would be to become a member of the church by moving our letter there. I don't know if moving our letter meant moving a physical letter, but we changed churches quite often, so our letter moved around quite a bit. When our parents decided to join a new church and move the letter, it would be necessary to make the decision publicly. This involved the whole family walking down to the front of the church during the invitation portion of the service and speaking to the pastor to let him know that we wanted to move our letter there. Membership cards and pencils with no erasers, in case you changed your mind, would be handed to each member of the family to fill out, then we would be seated on the front row of the church to await the vote of the congregation to determine if we were good candidates to move our letter there.

On this occasion, the membership cards were handed to all seven of us as we stood facing the congregation. Me and my four brothers reached into the deacons' hand to get a membership card at the same time and my head collided with my youngest brothers' head in mid reach. It felt like we hit heads pretty hard, I started seeing those little dots in my vision. I was glad when they told us to take a seat and wait for the vote.

The vote came in the form of "ayes and nays," and I don't recall hearing any nays so the letter must have moved again. I never understood how total strangers we never met can cast a vote about a family they never met, but nevertheless, the membership of the Second Baptist Church grew by seven that day.

My parents were faithful church attendees. Our letter must have arrived because my mom started teaching Sunday School and singing in the choir, and my dad made sure to get us to Sunday School on time. He would shine all our shoes and line them up on the floor, usually sitting our shoes on the sports page of the newspaper so the residual shoe polish wouldn't stain the linoleum. Dad would make sure we had our white shirts on with a bow tie or clip-on tie, depending on our age. We wore slacks, and belts that matched our shoes. Once dressed, my brothers and I would line up in front of the bathroom door to get our hair combed for church. Dad would start with hair oil, so much oil that if it was a hot day the oil would start to run down our foreheads and back of our necks. I figured that the reason we always wore white long sleeve shirts was to wipe the excess oil onto our shirt sleeves, which we did regularly. After oiling up our heads, he would start combing our hair. Each brother would sport sharply parted, fully oiled hairstyles. The comb Dad used was made of stainless steel with sharp teeth that made temporary grooves in our scalps. He would grip our foreheads with his free hand, preventing any movement, then tell us to hold still while near laceration occurred to our scalps from the steel comb. Once our eyes started to water, it would be time to comb the next head.

Dad would drive the family to Sunday School, drive back home and get himself dressed, then return to meet us at the church service. Dad would always show up in a suit, looking sharp. We were so proud of our dad. The only thing that kept him from looking perfect was the hair dye that he used on his prematurely graying hair as the green tint was evident in direct sun.

I ended up working up the nerve to make a public profession of faith in the Second Baptist Church. I walked publicly to the front of the church following one of my older brothers while thinking, "There is no way I am doing this by myself." We made our profession, then stood at the front of the church while the whole church came to the front to stand in a long line to congratulate us on our new-found Christianity. Dad had taught us to look all the men in the eye when shaking hands and to grip their hands, not too tight or too loose. Dad would say, "No respectable man wants to shake hands with a limp fish." All the older women wanted to hug us, which was fine with me. I figured it was a fair enough trade: having to smell all their stinky perfumes swapped for hair oil smeared all over their clothes.

The church now had our membership letter and two more professions of faith that year to add to the running tally. Now it was time for the baptisms, which were also counted and posted in the church bulletin.

The baptisms were usually scheduled at the end of the evening services. The deacons tell you to wear a colored t-shirt so people can't see through it when coming up out of the water and to bring a towel to dry off. My older brother went in the water with the pastor first, while I waited in the wings. The pastor wore chest-high fishing waders under a robe so he could stay dry and not soak the clothes he just preached in. The baptismal-tank water was supposed to be heated, or so they say, but no water heater was used that night. My older brother entered the water first, and since the water was so cold, his teeth started chattering immediately. He waded to the center of the tank where the congregation could see him through the glass portion of the tank that faced all the people. Baptism by immersion is a big deal in the Baptist Church. In order to determine and verify the authenticity of the proper depth of immersion, the tank has a transparent aquarium glass in the front. All the congregants in the church can see clearly through the glass to ensure the one being baptized is completely submerged.

I saw a yellow jacket wasp floating on the surface of the water when my brother entered the water, but before I could warn him, it stung him on the arm. He played it off well for a little boy, but I knew he was hurting. He came up out of the water and an attendant wrapped him in a towel and put cigarette tobacco on his sting. The man emptied the tobacco out of a couple of cigarettes and wrapped the tobacco in a paper towel. He wet the paper towel in the frigid baptismal water and pressed it on the yellow jacket sting to draw out the poison.

The attendant helping my brother took a big risk exposing his tobacco habit. Every Sunday, many of the church men would stand outside out of sight and smoke cigarettes acting as if no one could see them, but everyone did. During the late 1950s and early 1960s there were several taboo behaviors for upstanding Baptists: smoking, drinking alcohol, and dancing were three big ones, followed closely by hanging out with women who did.

To be considered part of the hierarchical upper echelon, dressing a certain way and maintaining hygiene was important, as well as position or status in the community. Attending church whenever the doors were open was also an unspoken requirement. The baptismal attendant, in the process of helping a little boy in pain from a sting that night, had exposed his own tobacco usage and hypocrisy but revealed his compassionate, benevolent heart in the process.

It was my turn next. I scanned the water, looking for the yellow jacket. Yellow jackets can sting multiple times, unlike a bee. I entered the arctic waters of the baptismal and was fully immersed as well. We now had our certificates of baptism as we had publicly expressed our faith in Christ through our desire to follow Him in baptism. We were official.

Some basic scriptures I had learned from childhood helped form who I would be in adulthood. "And they said, 'Believe in the Lord Jesus, and you will be saved, you and your household'" (*ESV Bible*, Acts 16.31). In Matthew, "Take my yoke upon you, and learn from me, for I am gentle and lowly in heart, and you will find rest for your souls. [30] For my yoke is easy, and my burden is light" (Matt. 11.29-30).

Knowing these timeless truths helped to positively shape my character. I would no longer subject myself to man-made rules that did not align with spiritual truths I knew and understood. At times, this would involve sifting through valuable sources of information only to select those truths in alignment with my spiritual belief system and subsequently discarding the rest.

Thank you, Mom and Dad

CHAPTER 2

Spiritual Journey

Our destination matters in life, but life is not found in the destination; life is found in the journey. The destination is only an end, an end to a goal or an end to a quest for something not yet obtained. At times, we arrive at a destination in life and immediately yearn again for the journey. Perhaps joy is to be found in the journey uphill, not the fleeting sense of satisfaction awaiting at the next peak.

The apparition occurred around 1980, forty-three years ago at the time of this writing. Why did it take so long to record? As I became much older and realized the impact the apparition would ultimately have on my life, I felt a need to record the events. Some people don't learn anything from the experiences of others. They must experience events on their own. Conversely, some do learn from the experiences of others. It is to these people that I write.

Like the Apostle Luke, the physician, who wrote the gospel of Luke: Luke wrote after Jesus had long been dead and resurrected, to give an account of the events of Jesus' life, for the benefit of others, so that they might know the truth. These same people, the ones who learn from the experiences of others, became the catalyst for recording the events of Christ's life.

At the time of the sighting, I couldn't possibly know how the apparition would affect my life as time passed. Now in retrospect, I can see the effect it has had on how I cognitively process life in my inter-actions with the world.

Sometimes, recognizing God's hand in the events of life can only come through hindsight. Many times, clarity is found after the fact, when all the pieces are in place. All I know is that when it happened, I remember thinking that it was so supernatural that if I went around sharing it with everyone, I would likely get faux interest and the eye roll behind my back. I basically kept silent, sharing only with my wife, who had already mastered the eye roll–so nothing new! She was present when the apparition occurred, only asleep. I tried to wake her to no avail. To this day I wonder what impact this would have had on her had she seen it as well.

At the time of the sighting, we lived in a middle-class residential neighborhood filled with houses of average, hard-working people. Our house was like all the other houses in the neighborhood. When we looked at buying the house, our realtor called the house a "great little starter home." I thought, "We must be slow starters." I believe the word used for this type of house is "cookie cutter," as each one on each street in the neighborhood had glaring similarities. Ours was on a cul-de-sac, right at the back. Anyone driving up our street would crash into our living room if their brakes failed.

We had purchased this three-bedroom, one-bath, 960-square-foot house in 1976, after getting married. Both of my wife's parents said we would never be able to pay for such an expensive house. It cost us $22,500.00 and our monthly payment was $202.00.

When we bought the house, I was working as an auto mechanic and my wife, a bookkeeper. We struggled financially, but the strug-gle, while difficult at times, was not out of the norm. This "scraping by" was part of life for the son of a hard-working, blue-collar worker. My father and mother, although great parents, never broke out of the lower-middle-class standing of society. Neither did my wife's parents. If we couldn't pay our own bills, our parents could not help us. We needed to manage life on our own. Fortunately, both of our parents raised us so that we would be able to manage life–never coddled, always striving without the benefit of a safety net. The only other person in our house that night was my one-year-old daughter, sleeping in her crib, which was rare for her. On most nights she would try to jump in the bed with her mom and me. I would get up and take her back to her crib, unless she was sick, then she would get a free pass to Mom's and Dad's bed.

Before getting married I had been living with my future spouse in her apartment and going to community college, which was paid for by the GI Bill. I worked part-time as a liquor-store cashier.

When we decided to get married, there was no church wedding for us. Her parents, not-so-staunch Catholics, but serious traditionalists, refused to set foot in a Baptist Church. The Catholic Church would not marry us because I would not agree to become a Catholic. We were married in a VFW hall. Shortly after getting married, I left the Baptist Church, and she left the Catholic Church. I quit my part-time, liquor-store job and college and took a full-time job as an auto mechanic.

One afternoon I was working at the automotive shop and my oldest brother stopped by. I hadn't seen him in a long time as he had been attending seminary on the east coast. We talked for a while then he asked me for twenty dollars. I gave him the money and he left. Later that same evening he stopped by my apartment and presented me with a brand-new Parallel Bible. Now I know why he wanted the twenty dollars. This Bible had four separate Bible versions together for study and comparison. He gave it to me and told me to start reading it in the New Testament, in the Gospel of John, so as not to get bogged down in Leviticus or Numbers in the Old Testament.

I started reading it after work, and so did my wife. After reading it for quite a while, I became aware of not just the reality of Jesus, but the terrible fallen nature of my own life. I had been living life as a successful sinner and was tired of the nihilistic nature of it all. Having already made a profession of faith as a little boy, professing to turn from sin and trust in God, I had made a sincere commitment to God but had not been living up to my end of the deal. I pondered the situation at length and determined that the difference between the commitment I made to God as a child, although authentic, lacked a clear understanding on my part of what put Christ on the cross in the first place: my sin.

What a horrific price Christ paid to redeem my soul. Yes, He paid for my sin with His life, I understood that as a young boy, but my concept of sin as a young boy did not fit with the innumerable malevolent atrocities mankind is capable of–that I am capable of.

To fully illustrate my naivete as a sixteen-year-old boy, I took a polygraph test before getting hired as a grocery bagger at our local grocery store. I finished the exam and asked the examiner if I had passed the test. He said that I had passed the test with flying colors. The worst infraction he could find was that I had been chewing gum while bagging groceries, which violated store policy.

Now at twenty-five years old, I prayed a prayer of faith, asked God to forgive my sinfulness, begged for a do-over, and put my faith and trust in Jesus instead of myself. God picked me up, dusted me off, and put me back in the game. I had shifted control of my life from my hands to God's.

According to my Bible, when we put our faith and trust in Jesus, we receive the promise of the Holy Spirit.

[13] In him you also, when you heard the word of truth, the gospel of your salvation, and believed in him, were sealed with the promised

Holy Spirit, [14] who is the guarantee of our inheritance until we acquire possession of it, to the praise of his glory" (Eph. 1.13-14).

So, according to scripture, I am now sealed with the promised Holy Spirit. In my life, this sealing by the Spirit has manifested itself in my newfound hunger for truth, specifically spiritual truth.

Shortly after my conversion experience, and feeling that nothing much had changed, I rode my motorcycle with my new wife to meet several of my friends at a bar to shoot some pool and drink some pitchers of beer. Nothing was different about this evening. I had a beer, played a little pool, then sat down at our table and ordered another pitcher. When the beer came, something changed.

I heard a voice, not an audible voice, but a quiet voice in my consciousness. The message was clear–simple and concise–you don't belong here. I immediately felt a physical heaviness on my shoulders, weighty and accompanied by a feeling that I needed to leave the bar. As soon as I left the bar, the heaviness subsided completely–evidence of the first change in my spiritual life.

My wife and I began attending a non-denominational church, very similar to a Pentecostal Church. Our belief system at that time, and still is, was to profess Jesus Christ as Lord and Savior for salvation through faith; however, I was not your model Christian. Actually, I believe there is no such thing as a model Christian, but I certainly had some growing to do.

I remember a church member visiting our house since we had filled out a visitor card at the church. He arrived unannounced; I had just gotten off work and was drinking a beer and cooking dinner in the kitchen. I remember I was not happy to see him and wished he would leave. My words were polite, but I'm certain he could sense that I was in no mood for his company, and he left.

Looking back at my ordinary life and considering the things that were happening at the time of the sighting, maybe my life was not ordinary at all. There were significant, stress-inducing life events and continuous struggles.

Ongoing financial struggles were exacting a stressful toll on us. At the time my wife and I had not received any financial training and were using credit cards at fast food places, which was unheard of in 1978. Buy a Big Mac on credit for two dollars at a twenty-four-percent revolving interest rate and you get to pay on it long after the hunger pangs are gone. Since the hunger always returned, there was never anything to show for the monetary outlay, except another credit card bill. When my wife's birthday came, her mother asked her what she wanted for her birthday. She told her mother that she really needed training pants to potty train our daughter because we didn't have money to purchase them. Money...was...tight.

Aiming at a better future, I left the auto-mechanic job and applied to become a firefighter with the city. It was a pay cut for me, but I would secure good medical benefits for my family. This point was driven home after becoming a firefighter. My crew and I would lead school demonstrations occasionally at the local elementary schools to teach students about fire safety. The young children seemed to care most about seeing the emergency lights and hearing the siren, but the older kids liked to see us handle hose lines and climb high ladders. While talking to a group of students, I asked them if they would like to be firefighters when they grew up which resulted in a resounding affirmation. I would then ask them why. A young third grader in the front row, waving his arm feverishly, replied, "Because you have a great dental plan!"

I only mention this career change because this decision resulted in reduced earnings in a time of already tight finances–stress compounded. Further stress occurred in my new job as I sought to try to prove my capabilities and abilities as a newbie. Being a cadet in the Fire Academy involved forty-hour-a-week training for six months–with no job security. Cadets are terminated for failure of any segment of the training.

The spiritual uncertainty I was experiencing was also causing stress. Knowing what I believed to be true spiritually, but basing assumptions on faith alone, was a precarious place to find myself–especially as I honestly hoped for a little clear evidence. So far, only the voice in my Spirit reminding me that I didn't belong in that bar was the only evidence I had. I needed to know why I believed what I was believing. I guess I really needed some affirmation that what I committed to believe by faith was truth.

I've heard pastors and Bible teachers say not to have a "hope so" type of faith, but to trust the scriptures to be true and live in confident faith. I do trust the scriptures, however, as a new Christian at the time, I really needed more than a pastor to say I just needed blind faith. Blind faith can be a dangerous undertaking. In 1978, more than nine hundred faithful church members of the Jim Jones congregation in the jungles of Guyana drank poison to demonstrate their faith–their blind faith. ("Jonestown"). Errant faith is still faith, but it is also still errant.

We all have a need to believe in something greater than ourselves. This type of belief is not blind faith, but an inner knowledge that we are not on top of the hierarchical ladder. We are created beings, not Creators. Ancient Hebrews referred to this pinnacle of the hierarchical ladder as Elohim, which means "Creator God." To have faith and live life passionately through faith is enough. We must take solace in this. Only in lived faith in Creator God can peace be found.

CHAPTER 3

Pre-Apparition

The financial struggles, coupled with a career change and the spiritual uncertainty I was experiencing, created a prime situation for a shake-up to occur. The apparition proved to be that shake up. If the apparition were truly meant for my eyes, and my eyes only, there would have to be an awareness of when I would be available to view it. It would also require a greater consciousness, a supernatural awareness, not of the natural world. A similar supernatural awareness can be found in the words of Jesus, the Christ. In the 1st century He spoke these words to His disciples, recorded in the gospel of Luke.

7 Then came the day of Unleavened Bread, on which the Passover lamb had to be sacrificed. 8 So Jesus sent Peter and John, saying, "Go and prepare the Passover for us, that we may eat it." 9 They said to him, "Where will you have us prepare it?" 10 He said to them, "Behold, when you have entered the city, a man carrying a jar of water will meet you. Follow him into the house that he enters11 and tell the master of the house, 'The Teacher says to you, Where is the guest room, where I may eat the Passover with my disciples?' 12 And he will show you a large upper room furnished; prepare it there." 13 **And they went and found it just as he had told them**, and they prepared Passover (Luke 22.7-13).

Another example of the supernatural awareness of Jesus and His words can be found in the gospel of Luke as well.

[28] And when he had said these things, he went on ahead, going up to Jerusalem. [29] When he drew near to Bethphage and Bethany, at the mount that is called Olivet, he sent two of the disciples, [30] saying, "Go into the village in front of you, where on entering you will find a colt tied, on which no one has ever yet sat. Untie it and bring it here. [31] If anyone asks you, 'Why are you untying it?' you shall say this: 'The Lord has need of it.'" [32] **So those who were sent went away and found it just as he had told them.** [33] And as they were untying the colt, its owners said to them, "Why are you untying the colt?" [34] And they said, "The Lord has need of it." [35] And they brought it to Jesus, and throwing their cloaks on the colt, they set Jesus on it (Luke 19.28-35).

Taking it a step further, assuming the apparition was for my eyes only, to be seen by me and nobody else, the apparition would require an awareness of where everyone in the house would be at that instance, in addition to knowing the location and current status of everyone who could possibly be able to see at that time: neighbors, a driver coming up the street, someone out walking their dog, or kids playing. There is always the possibility that the apparition is not only for my eyes, but was being viewed by others as well, with me being unaware of others present.

There is another possibility that the event could only be viewed by me, even if others were present. If this is true, there would be no way another person could see it, even if it was right in front of them. The scene would be visible to me and invisible to anyone else. Spiritually speaking, this is not unusual. Events such as these, where one person sees but others do not, are included in biblical history.

Recorded in the Old Testament of the Bible we see just such an account.

[15] When the servant of the man of God rose early in the morning and went out, behold, an army with horses and chariots was all around the city. And the servant said, "Alas, my master! What shall we do?" [16] He said, "Do not be afraid, for those who are with us are more than those who are with them." [17] Then Elisha prayed and said, "O Lord, please open his eyes that he may see." So the Lord opened the eyes of the young man, and he saw, and behold, the mountain was full of horses and chariots of fire all around Elisha (2 Kings 6.15-17).

God allowed Elisha to see the panorama in the sky, an army with horses and chariots of fire. Why did God allow Elisha to see and not the servant? We don't really know. What we do know is Elisha prayed for his servant and then his servant was allowed to see the spectacle in the sky.

Another example of this is found in the gospel of Luke. In the account, Jesus has been crucified, raised from the dead, and is walking on the road to Emmaus with two other men.

[13] That very day two of them were going to a village named Emmaus, about seven miles from Jerusalem, [14] and they were talking with each other about all these things that had happened. [15] While they were talking and discussing together, Jesus himself drew near and went with them. [16] **But their eyes were kept from recognizing him** (Luke 24.13-15).

We pick up the same account further along beginning in verse 28:

[28] So they drew near to the village to which they were going. He acted as if he were going farther, [29] but they urged him strongly, saying, "Stay with us, for it is toward evening and the day is now far spent." So he went in to stay with them. [30] When he was at table with them, he took the bread and blessed and broke it and gave it to them. [31] **And their eyes were opened, and they recognized him. And he vanished from their sight** (Luke 24.28-31).

I saw an apparition. To try to understand the reason, we need to work backward and determine the impact it had on me and process conclusions from there.

My wife and I had gone to bed at a typical hour, which was usually after the evening news, around 10:30 pm. Our daughter had already been put in her crib; it was just the two of us in the bed. There is nothing unusual at all about this evening. I don't remember the exact date, but I know it wasn't a holiday or any special calendar day. Just a routine day and a routine night. No celebrations had taken place that day. We didn't stay up late, as I said, just a routine night for an ordinary guy.

At around 4:00 am, in the early morning darkness, I was startled awake. I know the time because we had a clock radio alarm that displayed the time, although it wasn't set for any alarm. As I said, I worked shift work and didn't need to be at work until noon, and my wife was a stay-at-home mom since our daughter was born. I did not hear any noise; I did not wake up on my own. I was awakened, as if someone shook me to wake me up, but there was no one.

I immediately sat up in bed and moved to the head of the bed. There was a window behind the headboard–a window that was dusty because the shade stayed pulled as it faced the street. We never raised that shade. We lived in the house for ten years and I only remember raising the shade one other time to deter a would-be intruder.

On this night I reached over to behind the headboard of the bed and lifted the shade. From the time I was awakened, until the time I pushed the shade up behind the headboard, my actions seemed robotic. I had no thought to sit up in bed and to push open a shade that we usually never touched, but that is exactly what I did. Like being on autopilot, I was doing something I never did. *Why?* I've pondered these actions many times over the years with no answers.

I am a person that is intentional when it comes to actions. Prior to this night, I had spent three years in the Army and was now serving as a full-time firefighter in my city. I had been trained over the years to know and understand that what one does in training will be what one does in a real crisis. Preparedness, based on training, is how we learn to act decisively. Disciplined, self-controlled actions. Well-thought-out actions, rooted in routine. Without familiarity and training, fear can overcome actions. It seemed my actions on this night were happening to me.

CHAPTER 4

The Bridge

Looking out the window, I immediately saw a human-shaped figure facing me, standing in the cul-de-sac, slightly left of center. I had a small front yard, maybe twenty feet from my bedroom window to the street. The distance from the curb to the figure spanned another twenty feet–leaving me approximately forty feet from the figure.

I glanced at my wife still asleep soundly next to me. I called her name, she didn't budge. I called her name a little louder, but not loud enough to wake my daughter in the other room. She doesn't respond. I focused my eyes back on the unmoving figure in the cul-de-sac. I took my left hand to reach over and pinch my right arm. I felt pain–completely and totally awake. No fear overcame me. My mind told me to take a very good look. Take it all in. Focus on the figure. Study it.

It appeared like a human figure wearing a hooded robe. The figure was not giant or small, roughly the size of an average adult human. The hood was pulled up over where the head would be, hanging low in the front, around eye level on a human. I strained my eyes to see a face under the hood but couldn't see one. Where the face would be on a human, below the hood, was a medium gray, opaque space without form, almost as if the hood, which emitted its own dim white light, was causing the head area to be shaded. Never at any time was a face visible, only a hood pulled over the top of opaque, gray space with the dimensions of a human head, symmetrical to a human body. The robe was luminous, baggy, loose fitting, touching the ground, with loose sleeves covering what would be arms on a human body. No hands or feet were visible. The arms were hanging down on the sides of the body, as a human would stand. The robe itself was not transparent, but more like white clothing, with an opaque appearance. The robe emitted its own light, not bright, not blinding in any way, just enough to be easily visible at night. It's as if the brightness of the light was preset to reflect all the details of the apparition with a light comfortable enough for the human eye. The figure was motionless. We faced each other for what seemed like a long time, my eyes fixed, unblinking, staring, trying to make out a face where there is none. Time stood still.

Suddenly both arms moved upward and away from what would be the torso. The hands, if there were hands, were still not visible. Now the ends of the arms where wrists would be on a human, were outstretched on either side of the body, at eye level. The arms had a slight bend, as if there were elbow joints. The baggy sleeves hung loosely from the arms, glowing with the light emitted from the robe. My mind was not fearful but was telling me to check it out, watch it closely, take it all in. This was definitely not from this world. It held its arms up long enough for me to wonder what's next. It seemed to be prolonging the initial movement of the arms, holding the raised position for an extended amount of time. It's as if the apparition was making sure I got the best possible look at what was happening. Slowly the arms dropped back to the sides of the body. The figure appeared as when I had first seen it. *Now what?*

CHAPTER 5

Fear and Movement

S tanding, still facing me with the arms now down by its sides, it started to move positions. Until now it had been stationary, just left of the center in the cul-de-sac. Suddenly it appeared to walk like a human, its arms moved slightly back and forth. The speed of movement–like a big-city, lunch-hour, pedestrian on the sidewalk–was not a stroll, but not a fast walk either. The head did not move up and down while walking, but remained in the same level position, stable and unmoving. It's almost like the apparition was gliding over the cement surface of the cul-de-sac. There were approximately forty feet between the original position of the figure and the window I was peering through, only now, the figure was moving directly toward me. After the figure moved ten feet, I started to get anxious. Another ten feet in my direction and it would reach the grass in my front yard. It kept moving straight in my direction without altering its course. Now my anxiousness gave way to fear, not severe enough for me to try to get away, as if I could, but enough to make me aware that if there was no change in direction, this could all end badly for me. I held my position at the window. It had now walked about twenty feet in my direction. I still couldn't make out a face. The posture of the figure hadn't changed. It moved without pause, steadily, standing straight and tall, no slumping, head erect.

After the figure closed the gap about twenty feet, it changed course. As soon as it reached my lawn, much to my relief, it turned left approximately ninety degrees and continued in an almost perpendicular direction from the direction it was traveling. I was perplexed. Why would the figure move in a path at a ninety-degree angle instead of taking a short cut diagonally across the cul-de-sac from where it had been standing? It made no sense in my mind. When walking somewhere I tend to take the shortest route to where I am going. We all do. Pondering this later, I concluded that the only reason for it to take the relatively sharp left turn might have been twofold: to come close enough to me to give me an extraordinarily good look at it, and secondly, to alleviate any fear I might have been experiencing, which I admit, had started to swell in intensity.

The figure's new course had it headed toward a house, not the house next to my house, but two doors down. This change in direction had not only given me a vantage point that allowed me to see the side profile of the image, but it also allowed me to notice something fascinating. As it moved across my front lawn at a steady pace, I noticed the gown, still emanating light as before, moved outward at the level where knees would have been, indenting the gown with the imprint a knee would make, alternating on either side of the front of the gown, as if a human were wearing the gown and walking. Still no hands or feet were visible, as I watched the side profile of the figure moving steadily across my lawn. No fear was in my mind at this point, only curiosity.

Where was it going? Was it coming back? What would happen if it returned?

My eyes were focused on the rear of the image as it had passed in front of me now and was moving away from me. The same steady pace, not bouncing, it appeared to glide across my neighbor's lawn. Twenty feet away from me, thirty feet, forty feet, it was now approaching the front of my neighbor's house. The pace continued, unaltered. It reached the front of the house. The wall on the front of the house had a brick veneer wrap about eight-feet tall. I watched as the figure reached the front of the house and was gone, it vanished while I watched.

CHAPTER 6

Questions

I closed the window shade and looked at my wife, still asleep. I laid back down. Forget sleeping. My eyes could not close, my brain would not shut off. I laid in bed, trying my best to process everything. None of this made any sense. I had just seen something that doesn't exist in our world—but it does. I had seen with my own eyes. *How do I even begin to tell anyone about this? Why would I tell?* The next morning, I told my wife. She believed me but had little to no response, like telling your best friend that you are really an alien from outer space. What kind of response would I have if someone I knew well told me about this? Exactly. I mentioned it to a few close friends and family over the years with similar responses, not that they didn't believe me, it's just far too supernatural to fully process. When dealing with the subjective spiritual realm, explanations are near impossible. Dr. Jordan Peterson explains this belief without science in his book, *Beyond Order: 12 More Rules for Life.*

It could be, instead, that the value of something is sufficiently idiosyncratic, sufficiently dependent on the particularities of time, place, and the individual experiencing that thing that it cannot be fixed and replicated in the manner required for it to exist as a scientific object. This does not mean, however, that value is not real, it means only that it is so complex that it cannot yet and may never fit itself within the scientific worldview (Peterson 165).

If Dr. Peterson's evaluation of value, subjective value, as being very much a reality even apart from scientific objectivity is true, this might help explain what I encountered.

What have I learned from the apparition? A spiritual realm exists. It exists, if seeing is believing. I have seen clear evidence; I just don't know anything else about it. The real question is whether seeing is believing. For me, it is. Seeing it was enough for me to be convinced.

CHAPTER 7

Changed

Have I changed because of the sighting, and if so, in what way? I don't understand much about the world we live in, but I now know that there is more to it than we can see in the physical realm. I can relate to Thomas, a disciple of Jesus, recorded in history.

24 Now Thomas, one of the twelve, called the Twin, was not with them when Jesus came. 25 So the other disciples told him, "We have seen the Lord." But he said to them, "Unless I see in his hands the mark of the nails and place my finger into the mark of the nails, and place my hand into his side, I will never believe (John 20.24-25).

Many refer to Thomas as "doubting Thomas." Thomas declared that part of his being able to believe that Jesus was alive after Jesus' crucifixion would require him seeing a living Jesus with his own eyes. He did.

To Thomas, being able to see something helped bring it into his reality, the reality of existence by sight, specifically his sight. He had to see, for trusting others' testimony seemed to fall short.

Viewing something seemingly supernatural in a totally conscious state, fully awake, is life changing. This was an actual physical encounter with the spiritual. I distinctly remembered intentionally pinching my own arm. I felt real pain. I wanted to rule out any possibility of this being anything other than an encounter with something supernatural. This happened in real time. Not only did I see clear evidence of the spiritual realm, the appearance of the apparition convinced me that there was unquestionable evidence that **I am also seen**. I had been shown something not from this world by Someone described in scripture as **El Roi, the God who sees me**. Genesis 16, is the only place in scripture that the Hebrew word, "El Roi," appears.

[1] Now Sarai, Abram's wife, had borne him no children. She had a female Egyptian servant whose name was Hagar. [2] And Sarai said to Abram, "Behold now, the Lord has prevented me from bearing children. Go in to my servant; it may be that I shall obtain children by her." And Abram listened to the voice of Sarai. [3] So, after Abram had lived ten years in the land of Canaan, Sarai, Abram's wife, took Hagar the Egyptian, her servant, and gave her to Abram her husband as a wife. [4] And he went in to Hagar, and she conceived. And when she saw that she had conceived, she looked with contempt on her mistress. [5] And Sarai said to Abram, "May the wrong done to me be on you! I gave my servant to your embrace, and when she saw that she had conceived, she looked on me with contempt. May the Lord judge between you and me!" [6] But Abram said to Sarai, "Behold, your servant is in your power; do to her as you please." Then Sarai dealt harshly with her, and she fled from her.

[7] The angel of the Lord found her by a spring of water in the wilderness, the spring on the way to Shur. [8] And he said, "Hagar, servant of Sarai, where have you come from and where are you going?" She said, "I am fleeing from my mistress Sarai." [9] The angel of the Lord said to her, "Return to your mistress and submit to her." [10] The angel of the Lord also said to her, "I will surely multiply your offspring so that they cannot be numbered for multitude." [11] And the angel of the Lord said to her, "Behold, you are

pregnant and shall bear a son. You shall call his name Ishmael, because the Lord has listened to your affliction. [12] He shall be a wild donkey of a man, his hand against everyone and everyone's hand against him,and he shall dwell over against all his kinsmen." [13] So she called the name of the Lord who spoke to her, **"You are a God of seeing," for she said, "Truly here I have seen him who looks after me"** (Gen. 16.1-13).

Over forty years have passed since seeing the apparition. If asked whether my life has been different having seen the apparition, the answer would be a clear, definitive yes. How do I know? Because the life events that unfolded over the forty years after would have been nearly impossible to navigate successfully–and by successfully, I do not mean being victorious over every situation with positive outcomes–without the fundamental knowledge that there is more to this life than the physical realm. I needed to know this. Even though there have been setbacks, trials, tribulation, and hurt, there has always been the knowledge of something more to carry me forward with hope. This was life changing. Witnessing a sight not from our physical world confirms the existence of something more than our physical realm. The spiritual realm is very much alive, of this I am totally convinced.

I was awakened again, months after the sighting, this time from the sound of gunfire at around 4:00 am. I got ready to go to work the next day and saw four bullet holes in my neighbor's front door. At the time, with me being gone at work every third night, I didn't feel it was safe for my family to continue to live in our first house, so we moved from the little house that will forever be connected to the sighting.

The new house was a double-wide mobile home we purchased. We had it moved to two acres of treed land located about twenty miles from the big city where I worked full time for the Fire Department. It was peaceful. No more gunshots in the middle of the night.

Changing my address did not cause my spiritual hunger to subside, if anything, it was intensifying. I could not piece it all together yet, but it seemed I would be forever changed. The charismatic church we were attending in the city was not fulfilling the spiritual hunger I was experiencing. Living in truth will not allow an imposter like shallow faith to survive. Shallow faith, a meager faith, is anemia. One has confident faith, weak faith, or no faith. Jesus talks about this weak faith to the church in Laodicea:

[14] To the angel of the church in Laodicea write: These are the words of the Amen, the faithful and true witness, the ruler of God's creation. [15] I know your deeds, that you are neither cold nor hot. I wish you were either one or the other! [16] So, because you are lukewarm—neither hot nor cold—I am about to spit you out of my mouth. [17] You say, 'I am rich; I have acquired wealth and do not need a thing.' But you do not realize that you are wretched, pitiful, poor, blind and naked (Rev. 3.14-17).

Did David have confident faith when facing Goliath?

[44] The Philistine said to David, "Come to me, and I will give your flesh to the birds of the air and to the beasts of the field." [45] Then David said to the Philistine, "You come to me with a sword and with a spear and with a javelin, but I come to you in the name of the Lord of hosts, the God of the armies of Israel, whom you have defied. [46] This day the Lord will deliver you into my hand, and I will strike you down and cut off your head. And I will give the dead bodies of the host of the Philistines this day to the birds of the air and to the wild beasts of the earth, that all the earth may know that there is a God in Israel (1 Sam. 17.44-46).

My experience with this charismatic church was not even close to what I thought living an authentic life fully, in spiritually deep truth, could be. My desperate search began.

CHAPTER 8

The Adventure Begins

Things were going okay at work. I graduated from the six-month Fire Academy and had been assigned to a "working" firehouse just east of downtown. I found out later why it was aptly named a "working" firehouse. Being a rookie, I wasn't aware of the stark difference in firehouses in the city. The firehouses close to the city center were "working houses" because of the high number of emergency calls per shift. The firehouses in the suburban areas of the city were known as "country clubs" because they responded to far fewer calls. Firefighters would say that the wheels on the fire engines in country clubs had spider webs in the wheel wells because they hardly ever rolled.

My assignment brought me to an old fire house built in the 1920s–two stories with the bunk room on the second floor and a combination day room/dining room/kitchen on the first floor. An antique, horse-drawn steam fire engine sat in the corner of one bay. The first thing I noticed was that the TV in the corner of the dining room had a heavy iron strap that was bolted on the TV to secure it to a built-in table. I soon learned that it had to be bolted down because people called in false alarms in our neighborhood so they could come into the firehouse and steal the TV while no one was in the station.

When emergency calls came in, we would slide down one of two poles and jump on the fire engine. Sliding the pole and landing on the first floor required moving away from the pole quickly or risk having the next sliding firefighter land on your head. Once on the first floor we would move as fast as possible to jump onto the fire engine, which would be parked inside the firehouse. If the fire engine, also called the apparatus in the 1980s, was left outside on the front ramp too long, the equipment mounted on the apparatus such as fire axes and brass nozzles would grow legs and walk off, never to return.

Before climbing on the apparatus, it was necessary to jump into bunker boots and pull up the bunker gear pants. The pants were already pulled down and bloused around the top of the boot legs. Next came the suspenders which were thrown up over the shoulders while grabbing the bunker coat hanging on the side of the apparatus. Once the bunker coat was on, we climbed on, sat down facing backward in the open air jumpseat and put on helmet and gloves. If the call came in as a structure fire, the breathing apparatus and mask would be donned on the way without going on bottled air. Bottled air would be saved for use later on scene.

Sitting facing backwards while racing to the scene of a structure fire with emergency lights flashing and siren blaring became the ultimate adrenaline experience that I never tired of after many years of firefighting. Readying for a fire felt like going into battle with a naturally occurring, thermal enemy that destroyed property and killed innocent people indiscriminately.

Sitting in a jump seat with one shoulder touching the aluminum cover that protected the diesel engine was a gift and a curse. In the summer the heat radiating off the engine compartment provided additional heat to an already sweaty experience. On cold winter days, we would unlatch the cover and raise it up while going down the road. This allowed the engine to be exposed, which radiated heat to warm the otherwise frigid jump seat.

The working firehouse where I was assigned was close to railroad yards that divided our fire district. The rail yards were built first, so a concrete bridge was constructed over all the sets of railroad tracks to allow vehicle traffic to cross the yards. Most of our structure fires required us to drive over the quarter-mile-long bridge over the rail yards. Once we would crest the high point of the bridge our officer riding in the cab facing forward, would have a vantage point to view most of our district. If he saw heavy smoke or fire while crossing the bridge, he would turn around and beat on the plexiglass partition separating the rear jump seats from the cab so we could get our gear ready for action. We would then turn on our breathing tank, but not don the mask yet. Many times I would turn around enough to see out the front windshield, to see if I could catch a glimpse of the fire from the bridge. If it was a cold night, my officer would put on a leather, fleece-lined head covering that covered his ears and snapped under his chin, then put his helmet on. I used to tease him about his headgear because it looked like the headgear the Japanese kamikaze pilots wore in World War II. Once the leather headgear went on, I knew we were in for a firefight.

There was always something surreal about seeing the flames in the distance on a dark night. Knowing our imminent destination, wondering if everyone had gotten out in time, and mentally preparing for the possibility of a rescue, I would watch the slow-motion dance of the flames in the sky. The siren wailed, the air horn blared, the radio barked sounds that could not be understood over the sound of the diesel engine roaring. The chaos of the present moment opposed the hypnotic dance of the distant flames. There was nothing in the world that could top this. I was made for this.

My firehouse consisted of a fire crew of four on an engine and two paramedics on one ambulance. The ambulance, along with eleven other ambulances throughout the city covered the whole county–at the time about 1.5 million people. I was assigned to the fire crew. The city at that time had about a million residents. I was assigned to a district where residents were living in abject poverty. A large portion of our response district consisted of failed government housing projects that bred generational poverty. We referred to these housing projects as "courts." We responded to most of our emergency calls in the courts.

The rest of the fire calls were to residents in old wood-frame houses, mostly one story, but graduating to two and three story on the edge of downtown. They burned fast and hot.

Looking back, I realized how fortunate I was to be assigned to a working firehouse and on a crew with a seasoned officer in charge. He was no nonsense when it came to firefighting. As a rookie, when I first joined his crew, he told me that I better not ever be seen on TV at a big fire. If he saw me on TV, it meant I wasn't pulling my weight inside the burning structures. He valued interior firefighting, working from inside the structures. If there were any way he could get inside to put the fire out and perform rescue he would. He despised what he called sidewalk firefighters. These firefighters demonstrated no courage and would choose to stand outside the burning structures and spray water from safety.

I get it, some structures are too far gone or heavily damaged to the degree that it is impossible to get inside. If there were a slim chance to get inside and conduct a rescue or extinguishment, my officer would go for it. He would always tell me that he better never turn around and not see me right behind him while working inside. He wanted me to stick with him like glue. I did.

Early on, I learned that he had quite a reputation as one of the best firefighters in the city. We were called out for a fire at an old two-story restaurant bar with fire on the second floor. We pulled up in front to find two other fire companies already on scene. The first floor was already pumping heavy black smoke from the front door and windows. Fire was engulfing the upper floor. He told me to pull a preconnect line with a fog nozzle. A preconnect is a line that is already connected to the pump panel of the fire engine so the line can be charged with water from the tank on board the fire engine as soon as the officer gets in place with the nozzle. We stretched the line to the front door and charged it with water. Two or three firefighters from the other companies were standing in front of the front door spraying water on the smoke coming out the front door. This does nothing.

My officer pushed them out of the way and we went in the front door in search of the interior stairwell. I pulled the line and stuck to him like glue while he handled the nozzle. Visibility was zero, it started to get warm, no, hot. He found the interior stairwell somehow, and we started going up. So far, we hadn't sprayed a drop of water. The stairs were difficult to navigate, as charred wood and burning embers rained down on both of us. We got to the top of the stairs and he opened the nozzle. He directed the nozzle while I handled the back pressure from the line. He put the fire out with less than five hundred gallons, the amount of water we carried on the engine. We took the line back down the stairs and exited the building.

The Chief met us outside in the parking lot and told us we did a good job. He told us to just pick up our line and head back to the station. The Chief was going to get the other firefighters to do salvage and overhaul, stripping the walls in search of hot spots. It was that day, early on, that I knew that our fire crew was one of the best on the shift. The other companies knew it as well, and so did the Chief.

I learned rather quickly why our's was deemed a working firehouse. It was now 4:00 am, the trip fell, signaling a structure fire. This one was close to our firehouse, so we were the second engine to arrive on scene. A city block from the scene we turned a corner onto the street where the fire was. Still a hundred yards from the fire, I put my face shield down covering my face to shield my face from the heat. The heat was coming from a three-story, wood-frame house fully involved with fire that had ignited the three-story wood-frame house next to it. The second house was fifty percent involved in fire, and a third house, equally as large as the other two, was catching fire from the radiant heat. The first fire engine on scene caught a fire hydrant on the corner. They began laying big lines but were forced to abandon their location–too close to the fire. The taillight lenses on the back of the fire engine were melting, as well as their hose bed cover. They had to reposition further back from the heat.

My officer called for a big line and a twenty-four-foot extension ladder. There were no savable occupants in the first two houses, the fire was too extensive. My officer wanted to knock down the fire enough on the third house to get inside and check for occupants. I ran back to our fire engine to retrieve a ladder. A detail man, a man that has been sent from another station to work on our fire crew, was with me. A detail man was used to fill in when another firefighter was on vacation or unable to work for various reasons. To get the ladder off the side of the fire engine it was necessary to release the ladder locks. Turning two handles would accomplish the task, with one man on either end of the ladder. I grabbed my end and unlocked it. For some reason the other firefighter had started to panic. It was hot and chaotic, but he's a firefighter. I yelled at him to turn the handle. He couldn't. It was not for lack of strength, he was a big, muscular guy.

Something else was going on mentally or emotionally. I yelled at him a second time. He tried to force the ladder off the fire engine using brute strength. He was rocking the whole fire engine back and forth. I went to his ladder lock and turned the lock to release it. I looked at his eyes and he looked like a wild man, scared and confused with wild eyes. I took the ladder off the fire engine by myself and returned to my officer who had managed to always work on a fine line between total success and utter disaster.

My officer had experienced disaster before, at another fire, but survived relatively unscathed aside from soreness. That time, he was trying to get off the burning roof of a two story house. The fire had broken through the roof so fast that a roof collapse was quick and imminent. He tried to quickly get off the roof by grabbing an extension ladder that was leaning against the roof. The ladder had been set up hastily from the ground and had not been locked properly, so as soon as he stepped foot on the ladder, it began to collapse. He began his freefall from the second story roof, falling in a supine position with his breathing apparatus tank on his back being closest to the ground. Another firefighter on the ground saw him falling and managed to throw his shoulder into his falling body to cushion his fall before he hit the ground. Had it not been for the heads up reaction from the firefighter on the ground, my officer would have possibly sustained serious injuries. He was saved by a brother doing what the brotherhood does.

He had managed to pull the big line single handedly in the twenty-foot-wide space between the second and third houses. He was already in a near inferno, focusing his hose stream on the third house, using it as a water curtain to save as much of the third house as possible to allow entry. He turned and yelled at me to keep an eye on the fire from the second house, and to let him know if it got too close. I acknowledged. I also knew his standard of close and my standard of close were two very different assessments. I was behind him, helping him handle the back pressure of the line, while I watched the flame from the second house, now three feet from lapping on my bunker coat. I didn't tell him yet, but it was getting crazy. The fire kept winning, but he held his position. We stayed in position for maybe ten more minutes before we saw any progress. Slowly the game shifted in our favor. More troops arrived, a thorough interior search was initiated, and everyone was found safe. The firefighter who had so much trouble with the ladder locks was found lying on the ground, face down in the mud. It turned out he had acquired a recent drug addiction. He was killed not many days after this fire by a gunshot wound to the face before he could ever be fired by the Fire Department.

We finished up at the scene, uncoupled and drained all the water out of the hose lines, then repacked the dirty hose on the hose bed on the back of the fire engine. We packed it in such a way that it was immediately ready to deploy if we caught another fire before we returned to the station. The sun was rising higher in the sky as we made the short drive back to the firehouse. The dirty hose was pulled off the fire engine, scrubbed down and rinsed, then hung on the thirty-foot hose tower behind the firehouse to dry. Clean, dry hose was pulled out of the storage bins and repacked on the hose bed on the fire engine. It was close to the noon shift change. We had just enough time to clean the kitchen and restrooms, sweep and mop the floors and the bay while the driver washed the fire engine. We finished cleaning the fire station and helped the driver chamois the fire engine dry before our relief crew walked in the station. No breakfast today, time to go home to the family.

A firefighter in a working firehouse lived most shifts in a state of extremes, from adrenal overload to exhaustion. For this reason, I came home sleep deprived and exhausted most shifts. When asked how the shift was after I walked in the front door at home, it was difficult to say anything other than, "Fine." Home was another world, a safe comfortable place juxtaposed against life in a working firehouse.

No one but firefighters in working firehouses can truly understand the world a firefighter lives in for twenty-four hour increments every forty-eight hours. Some shifts required a certain amount of winding down at the end of a shift before trying to steer a car home without falling asleep at the wheel.

At the end of many shifts, the crew would take off their badge shirts and drive to the icehouse down the street that had picnic tables outside where we sat and had a couple of beers together. We didn't speak much, just stared at the traffic going by as we picked at the labels on our beer bottles. One by one we got up, rubbed our red eyes, already red before opening our first beers, slapped hands, and drove away.

Arriving home, dead tired, I would lie in bed in an exhausted stupor, a poor substitute for restful sleep. Having fought sleep for so long, now my red eyes wouldn't close, and sleep was elusive. Eventually, a black stupor would take over, no dreams, just drooling blackness. My wife would not allow my toddler daughter to play with daddy until I woke up from my sleep. I did not find out until my oldest daughter was grown that she used to sit outside my bedroom door watching the door handle to see when it would turn and I would emerge. Three to four hours later, I would be up for the day. The brain stayed hazy, still tired, no motivation to do anything with the remainder of the day. My feet would hit the floor, I would stagger to the shower and try to clear the stubborn haze. I had a love-hate relationship with my job.

CHAPTER 9

Sunday Masks and the Church's "F" Word

We received a local newspaper in the mailbox at the new house. A local church in the area, a Baptist church, advertised in this paper, "We preach Jesus, and the drive is worth the difference." We decided to give it a try, even though I was done with the man-made laws that many traditional denominations try to impose on their congregants.

We drove to the new church on Sunday. It seemed like a country church, rural, with about two hundred people. The pastor emphasized salvation by faith in Christ and His finished work on the cross. I get it, I believe it by faith as well, but for me the sighting seemed to have placed a deep spiritual hunger in me that would either reinforce what I currently believed or steer me in another direction.

As the New Testament scripture penned by the Apostle Paul, in Romans points out: so **faith** comes from **hearing**, and **hearing** through the word of Christ (Rom. 10.17).

It's one thing to believe something to be true by learning about it and studying it further. It's quite another thing to personally witness the reality of the supernatural. It seemed I needed to know more. The sighting had caused a burning passion for more in me.

The people at the church were nice, although many seemed pharisaical, still struggling with a salvation-by-good-works belief system with which many church people struggle. It goes like this: "If only I could stop sinning and act better and do more good deeds, God would love me more." This is the kind of false belief system under which many live. Acknowledging the fact that we are all sinners, and that Christ died on the cross to pay the penalty for our sin, doesn't align with trying to act right and fix ourselves. If that were the case, we would have no need for a Savior. The great lie that Satan tries to place on us is that we are all basically good, that we are just fine the way we are, and we just need to keep trying to do good deeds. This is a huge deception. We are not just fine, and we are not good. We are capable of doing good and also the most evil, malevolent things imaginable.

[21] For from within, out of the heart of man, come evil thoughts, sexual immorality, theft, murder, adultery, [22] coveting, wickedness, deceit, sensuality, envy, slander, pride, foolishness (Mk 7.21-22).

This word from Mark reminds me of Alexander Solzhenitsyn's thoughts about the line between good and evil in his book, *The Gulag Archipelago*:

"The line separating good and evil passes not through states, nor between classes, nor between political parties either — but right through every human heart —and through all human hearts. This line shifts" (Solzhenitsyn 312).

Aleksander Solzhenitsyn spent thirteen years as a prisoner in the gulags under the evil rule of Joseph Stalin. The gulags were work camps located throughout the Archipelago in Russia. It has been estimated that sixty million people died in Russia during Stalin's rule. We, like Stalin, are all capable of good and evil.

The church services for the good and evil people were on Sunday morning and evening, and a Wednesday night prayer meeting. Several men's and women's Bible-study groups met before the Sunday-morning service, as well as adult couples' Bible study classes. We had two children by this time, so we placed them in their appropriate classes by age, and my wife and I started attending one of the adult couples' classes. This study class felt like a new journey to us. We were like sponges ready to absorb any new spiritual knowledge. The teacher was a nice man. He had a wife and three young children. When we got to church, he would ask me how I was doing and I would not answer with the traditional, denominational "F" word: "Fine," but would tell him that my kids fought in the backseat all the way to church. His reply would be, "Mine, too." Refreshingly real.

He was a decent teacher, mild mannered, dogmatic, and polite, but too Baptist. His opinions would never stray outside denominational lines. I could learn from him, but he could only take me to the limits of Baptist doctrine, with no chance of wading into the deep end. He said he believed angels were real, but if he ever saw one, I'm fairly certain he would go into cardiac arrest on the spot. Because of the sighting, I wanted more.

The people in the class were nice. They were mostly new Christians who professed faith in Christ as long as it didn't interfere with their personal lives. If Jesus' teachings didn't fit their paradigm, they simply ignored His words and played church. Being surrounded by beautiful stained glass windows didn't alter the basic human condition of mankind. We were all still struggling with the balance of good and evil within our own hearts.

I developed relationships with many of the people in the church. Aside from a few exceptions, most were well intentioned, personable, likable, giving, friendly people. They wanted to be "good Christians." Much of their free time was spent doing good deeds whenever possible and simultaneously concealing the fact that they were not following all the Baptist, man-made traditions. Being real and not following man-made traditions would take courage. Instead of destroying their status in the church by ignoring man-made tradition, they remained silent, wearing their Sunday masks.

CHAPTER 10

Firefighter Life

B etween responding to fire calls, the firefighters bunked out on the second floor in the evenings. We all slept in one open room, except for the fire officer, who had an office with a bunk in a separate room. The two paramedics had their own bunk room as well but were rarely at the firehouse. The paramedics all swore that there was a sensor inside their pillowcase that set off the alarm for another emergency call as soon as their head touched their pillows.

After midnight on nights with a full moon, or the end of the month, or a weekend, it was especially busy. The full moon increased the number of emergency calls, to this day I don't really know why, but we were aware of a definite pattern. The end of the month, or the first of the month was when all the government checks were issued, social security disability, unemployment checks, and other monetary income. In several of the homes in our fire district, the first dollar was spent on alcohol, drugs, or to pay back the money borrowed to make it to the end of the month. End-of-the-month weekends were especially busy. The ones who worked were sometimes off from work on the weekend and ready to get crazy with a paycheck in their hands. Hot weather would also increase emergency calls. In our response neighborhood, people who could afford cars, typically drove cars with no air conditioning. The air conditioner would break and there was no money to fix it. Traffic congestion, 100-degree heat, challenging living conditions, and no end in sight to their misery created unbelievable road rage. Otherwise respectful citizens living in these conditions could turn into raging, out-of-control monsters when another vehicle would cut in front of their car.

On hot summer nights the people in houses and living in the courts were out on their front porches. It would be too hot inside the house so everyone was outside, including the children. It was not unusual to see young children playing outside around the dumpsters at 2:00 am. This phenomenon created an uncommon social dynamic between everyone, parts good, and some not so good.

One of the members of my fire crew was promoted and left for another assignment. A brand-new rookie showed up to take his place, which meant I was no longer the rookie. He seemed like a good fit, willing to learn, and knowing that the drill academy taught him fundamentals but nothing else that would prepare him for where he was now. His first shift with us was a hot day, as most were.

Our officer put him in full bunker gear with a breathing apparatus on his back. He gave him a fifty-foot section of hose to rickrack over his shoulder and had him climb up and down the thirty-foot hose tower in the back of the firehouse. A hose tower was used to hang dirty firehose to dry after washing. After several trips up and down the tower he asked the officer for just a little break in the shade to catch his breath. Because of this request, his new nickname was aptly applied: Shade Break.

It got to be around midnight or 1:00 am; we were in our bunks waiting for our next call. Shade Break was in the bunk next to mine. He was worn out and snoring. In the dim light of the dorm, I saw the officer's door open. I could hear the officer sliding across the floor on his belly so no one could see him. He covered thirty feet or more on his belly and laid on the floor next to Shade's bunk. The officer was wearing a full wolf-head mask that covered his entire head. It had authentic-looking wolf hair all over it and an open mouth bearing big, snarling teeth. While still lying on the floor he reached up and grabbed Shade's arm and held on. Startled, Shade woke up. It was then that the officer raised his head high enough for Shade to see him. Hearing a grown man scream in sheer terror, like a little girl, at someone wearing a wolf head was one of the funniest things ever. Shade was one of us now.

Emergency calls were coming in steadily the entire shift; we were busy. All the emergency runs we responded to in our response area, coupled with the special requests for our presence in other areas of the city, made for a full shift. Since we had the best officer, the chief requested our services at many emergency scenes outside of our response area. It made our crew feel special and at the same time created jealous animosity among some of the firefighters at other stations.

The fire department would get called out for all calls for service where calling the police would not seem appropriate for the nature of the call. We were rolling for water rescues, body recoveries, recovering possible drowning victims, with their cars if applicable, trapped victims, vehicle accidents, jumpers trying to commit suicide, as well as the full range of fire-related calls. A call we never accepted was for cats stuck in a tree. A firefighter 911 dispatcher once told a lady who requested a fire crew to climb a tree to retrieve a cat, that we don't do cat-in-the-tree rescues. He followed up the reply with a question to the lady asking her if she ever saw a cat skeleton in a tree? Cats will climb down when they are ready.

The trip fell, which meant the alarm sounded in the firehouse for another emergency call. At the request of the Chief, we rolled out for a call that was out of our normal response area. It seemed there were a lot of firefighters already on scene at a creek that ran through the city. Apparently, there were witnesses that saw a young boy fall in the water and never resurface. The water was muddy so there was zero visibility.

We arrived and found firefighters dragging the creek with hooks tied to ropes randomly thrown in the water. This was going to be a body recovery, but so far no body had been found. The creek was about fifty feet wide, so my officer suggested we stretch a fifty-foot section of rope all the way across the creek and have the firefighters get in the water walking shoulder to shoulder. We could hold on to the rope and probe the bottom with pike poles. Pike poles are long poles with pointed hooks on the end primarily used for pulling down ceilings in burning structures.

We covered virtually every square foot of the creek bottom. I was positioned close to the middle of the creek. The maximum depth at the middle reached about five feet deep, so the water was never over my head. We had moved about fifty yards upstream when a firefighter standing next to me probed the body. I helped him bring the boy out of the creek and we laid him on the bank. He had been under the water too long for resuscitation efforts, but at least the closure his family would receive was worth our efforts. I was new to this type of rescue work, so on the ride back to the firehouse, I pondered why young children die before ever getting a chance to live, and conversely, why do others get to live long, full lives? Struggling to arrive at an answer, I soon realized there would be no answer. Who could possibly have an answer that made sense?

Not knowing there was more to life than what we see could create a hollow, hopeless, nihilistic approach to life that could deaden the soul. I started to understand the usefulness of witnessing the apparition and knowing that there was more to life than what we perceived in our day-to-day routines. It gave me hope. The apparition was evidence of a clear reality beyond this physical life on Earth.

The little boy having drowned, his physical body no longer living, was very much alive in his spirit. In the gospel of Luke, Jesus spoke to Sadducees who denied that there was any life after death. He reminded them of the conversation God, speaking from a burning bush, had with Moses. Abraham, Isaac, and Jacob, all who had died before the conversation between God and Moses, are spoken about as if they were still alive in spirit.

[27] There came to him some Sadducees, those who deny that there is a resurrection, [28] and they asked him a question, saying, "Teacher, Moses wrote for us that if a man's brother dies, having a wife but no children, the man must take the widow and raise up offspring for his brother. [29] Now there were seven brothers. The first took a wife, and died without children. [30] And the second [31] and the third took her, and likewise all seven left no children and died. [32] Afterward the woman also died. [33] In the resurrection, therefore, whose wife will the woman be? For the seven had her as wife."

[34] And Jesus said to them, "The sons of this age marry and are given in marriage, [35] but those who are considered worthy to attain to that age and to the resurrection from the dead neither marry nor are given in marriage, [36] for they cannot die anymore, because they are equal to angels and are sons of God, being sons of the resurrection. [37] But that the dead are raised, even Moses showed, in the passage about the bush, **where he calls the Lord the God of Abraham and the God of Isaac and the God of Jacob. [38] Now he is not God of the dead, but of the living, for all live to him."** [39] Then some of the scribes answered, "Teacher, you have spoken well." [40] For they no longer dared to ask him any question (Luke 20.27-40).

CHAPTER 11

New Teacher in Town

My wife and I continued to attend the little Baptist church. The sighting had created a hunger to find out as much as I could about spiritual things, the hunger was not going away, but if anything, getting stronger. I had become a truth seeker and developed a keen spiritual discernment, an ability to know when something being presented did not pass the smell test. I learned to sift what was taught, discard what seemed incorrect, and harvest the pearls of truth. I weighed what was taught against the truth discovered in the Bible. I became as the Bereans mentioned in the book of Acts.

10 The brothers immediately sent Paul and Silas away by night to Berea, and when they arrived they went into the Jewish synagogue. 11 Now these Jews were more noble than those in Thessalonica; they received the word with all eagerness, **examining the Scriptures daily to see if these things were so** (Acts 17.10-12).

I desperately wanted to know more.

After many months, maybe a year, of attending the adult Bible study class on Sundays, the teacher said he was going out of town and asked me to fill in as teacher the next Sunday. I told him I wasn't sure I could; I had issues with public speaking at the time. A pastor friend of mine once told me that most people would agree to walk over a bed of red-hot coals barefoot than to stand at a podium in front of people and speak. At the time, I could almost relate to that. Finally, after much coaxing, I agreed to give it a shot.

I studied the Biblical passages of scripture that I was to teach and expound upon, using the Baptist teaching material that provides the teacher an outline to follow. I was given the material a week in advance so I could prepare. The week went too fast for me, writing handwritten pages of notes to follow, coupled with my anxiety over public speaking, just about overwhelmed me before the weekend arrived. Finally, Sunday morning arrived, and I loaded the family in the car and made the drive with my misbehaving kids, to what felt like the crucifixion site, Golgotha, the place of the skull.

The class was scheduled to last an hour. I knew I needed to speak for most of the time, but my handwritten notes betrayed me. The more I looked at the notes the more I thought I might be able to burn through my notes in about ten minutes. As soon as I arrived at the church, feeling grossly unprepared to speak, a man came up to me and asked if I would fill in for their teacher as well since he was absent. His class was a men's class, and they were without a teacher. Their teacher had just told them to combine with the class I was going to teach. They did not know my teacher was out as well. The teacher for the largest adult couples' class had the same plan as well, he was out of pocket, expecting my teacher to fill in for him.

After the dust settled, I was expected to teach the combination of three classes, so we were moved to a big classroom with larger seating capacity. The big classroom had seats higher in the back of the room, sloping down to the front of the room so everyone could get a good view of me sweating. I stayed outside before the class began, away from anyone else who might decide they wanted a teacher at the last minute. Walking slowly on the sidewalk outside with my puny, handwritten notes, my Bible, a clean shirt that was once dry, and my dwindling confidence, I began to pray.

To me, the option of walking over red-hot coals barefoot instead of public speaking seemed a viable option worth pursuing at this point. After voicing a repetitive prayer to God consisting of me telling God over and over that I can't do this, something very strange happened. I heard a voice, not an audible voice, but a quiet voice in my sentient consciousness. The voice very clearly communicated, "No, you can't do it, but I can." This was the same voice I had heard a couple of years earlier when I was hanging out in the bar with my friends. I now recognize it as God's Spirit communicating with my spirit. Not a loud voice, but a quiet voice, not audible, but a voice meant only for me at this time.

It was a Moses moment. When God called Moses to lead the Israelites out of slavery in Egypt, Moses gave God excuses of why he couldn't do the task. He wasn't a good public speaker. God didn't let Moses off the hook and it appeared God isn't letting me slide either.

10 But Moses said to the Lord "Oh, my Lord, I am not eloquent, either in the past or since you have spoken to your servant, but I am slow of speech and of tongue." **11** Then the Lord said to him, "Who has made man's mouth? Who makes him mute, or deaf, or seeing, or blind? Is it not I, the Lord? **12 Now therefore go, and I will be with your mouth and teach you what you shall speak"** (Ex. 4.10-12).

I had been pacing on the sidewalk for about five minutes, still a nervous wreck, even after hearing God's voice. Calming my fear usually does not happen instantaneously, it's a process. The basis for removing fear is trusting the person trying to talk you off the ledge. If there is no trust, the fear refuses to subside. I finally decided to trust the voice and walked into the packed classroom.

A man was standing at the podium–stalling, waiting for a teacher to show up. He looked so relieved when I poked my head in the door. I was in a cold sweat, walking toward the podium, thinking, "I'm doomed for failure." I placed my Bible and my puny notes on the podium and a peaceful calmness came over me that I cannot explain. In retrospect, the calmness I had experienced when placing my Bible on the podium reminded me of a scripture where the Jordan River stopped flowing the moment the feet of the Levitical priests stepped into the river in an attempt to cross.

[15] and as soon as those bearing the ark had come as far as the Jordan, and the feet of the priests bearing the ark were dipped in the brink of the water (now the Jordan overflows all its banks throughout the time of harvest), 16 the waters coming down from above stood and rose up in a heap very far away, at Adam, the city that is beside Zarethan, and those flowing down toward the Sea of the Arabah, the Salt Sea, were completely cut off. And the people passed over opposite Jericho (Josh. 3.15-16).

God dried up the Jordan River the moment the priests' feet touched the water, not a minute sooner. God calmed my spirit the moment I laid my Bible on the podium, not a minute sooner. I had not even opened my mouth yet. I felt totally comfortable standing in front of all the people. I don't recall what I taught anymore, but people from the crowd approached me after the class and told me it was the best Bible teaching they had ever heard. I responded with a thank you, then gave God the credit. Interestingly, God did not let me off the hook until crunch time. He made me sweat it out until I knew I had to trust him, there was no other option; trust Him, or fail. I learned that I'm not the only one in the rescue business. Surrendering to trust in God was a huge catalyst to overcoming fear. It certainly was for me that day.

CHAPTER 12

Respect

Camaraderie, built by difficult, stressful working conditions, where the task at hand frequently overwhelmed abilities, evolved into a necessity during difficult fires. Trust was reinforced amongst the crew knowing that they had your back, and you had theirs. Violate that trust one time, and you became a firehouse pariah.

Firefighters' memories were acute when it came to remembering whether a partner left them hanging. They would remember that the crew member didn't have their back when things turned crazy and would make contingency plans to account for that fact in risk taking.

Firefighters are a brotherhood. Either you were in, or you were out—just like in the supper club. In busy firehouses all the firefighters would take turns cooking for the shift. When it was your turn to cook, dinner and breakfast were your responsibility. When I reported for duty on my first shift, I was told that I would cook when it was my turn, even if I didn't know how to boil water. I needed to learn. New cooks were always harassed about their cooking, even if it tasted delicious. Typically, when the food was served, one firefighter would say, "The food is missing something, but I can't quite figure out what it is." The other firefighters would reply, "Flavor," then they'd bust out laughing.

The only ones exempt from cooking were the paramedics on the ambulance. They were in the supper club but never had to cook. They responded to so many emergencies that they may never make it back to the firehouse during the whole twenty-four hour shift. Paramedics had a three-time microwave rule. When they tried to eat but would catch another emergency call, the firefighters would cover the paramedics' plates of food to keep flies off of it until they got back. When they returned and microwaved their food and caught another emergency call, we covered their food again. If this happened three times and they caught a third emergency call without eating, the paramedics wouldn't eat the food so it went in the trash, no longer edible.

Like brothers, firefighters would pick on one another mercilessly, but if an outsider lobbed an attack, there was hell to pay. In a busy firehouse the firefighters agitated and picked on each other constantly. The cardinal rule of effective agitation was that you must be able to take agitation before you were allowed to dish it out. If a firefighter tried to dish it out but couldn't take it, the other firefighters would jump on him like sharks in a feeding frenzy. Many a rookie who couldn't take the agitation probably reconsidered their career choice at one time or another. Unspoken, but true, was that the other firefighters wouldn't agitate anyone they didn't like or trust. They left these firefighters alone, with invisible labels, and ostracized–not a good position to be in if planning a long career.

There were multiple levels of agitation: ranging from mild, to over-the-top, and completely out of hand. Nicknames were commonplace among the firefighters and often spanned full careers. Several come to remembrance quite easily.

On this list was Blister. This was the firefighter that, like a blister, always showed up after the hard work was over.

And then there was Lobster, who got a tattoo of a scorpion on his stomach when he was young and fit. As he aged and gained weight, his scorpion tattoo began to look more like a lobster, and his nickname followed him his whole career.

Flounder liked to lay down and rest between emergency calls instead of hanging out in the dayroom doing other activities. The guys named him Flounder because they said that he laid on his side sleeping so much that it would eventually cause the eye farthest from his pillow to move to the lower side of his head, resembling a flounder's eyes.

In poverty, every day is a battle for survival, and many times the battle includes taking from others what is not theirs to take. Stealing and conning were prevalent in our response area. A fellow firefighter showed up at the firehouse with a TV he had just purchased in the neighborhood from a street hustler. He bragged about how he got such a good deal for a new TV still in the box. He only paid $50, and it was "still in the box, brand new."

His excitement waned when he opened the box and found only rocks in the box, enough rocks to weigh the same amount as a typical TV. At least two new things happened that day because of the transaction. The hustler had a new fifty-dollar bill, and the firefighter had a new nickname for life: Box of Rocks.

Firefighters like to "short sheet" each other's bunks. Typically, firefighters would put sheets on their bunks around 11:00 pm. When someone got "short-sheeted," a firefighter would go to the bunk room after the sheets are on the beds and remake the victim's bunk. One of the sheets is shortened to about three feet long, refolded and tucked under so it looks normal. The other sheet was left alone. When the unsuspecting victim returned from a fire, dead tired in the middle of the night, and tried to get in his sheets, he couldn't stretch out further than a cramped fetal position. His cursing would become equally as loud as the other firefighters laughing at him as he remade his bed.

Some firefighters brought snacks and sweets from home and put cold food in the firehouse refrigerator. Telling the other firefighters to leave your food alone opened the door for them to eat your snacks. One firefighter told everyone to leave his ice cream alone. Big mistake. The firefighters opened a small hole in the bottom of the container and ate all the ice cream from the bottom of the carton except for the top layer. They put the lid back on and put it back in the freezer as if it had been untouched. This served a couple of purposes. It sent a message to never tell the guys not to eat your stuff and served as a reminder to share what you have.

In the 1980s, the firehouses had gas stoves that operated with pilot lights instead of strikers. The top burners had pilot lights, as did the oven, usually in the back of the broiler near the floor. The firefighters would blow out the pilot light in the back of the broiler, turn the gas on full blast, then wait. Once the gas fumes accumulated sufficiently, a rookie would be called to help light the pilot light. Once the rookie put his head in the back of the broiler to relight the pilot light, the resulting gas explosion would usually singe his eyebrows, eyelashes and any other facial hair he might have. It's a higher-level agitation that taught rookies the dangers of gas explosions.

Throwing buckets of ice water on an unsuspecting firefighter while he showered was also a common form of agitation. So was throwing buckets of water from the second story windows to the firefighter on the ground. Catching rookies in a clean, dry uniform and soaking him to the bone was good training.

The worst agitation, where things were carried too far, happened to a firefighter who had bought a lotto ticket. While he was out of the firehouse on a call, the other firefighters managed to duplicate his lotto ticket to match the actual winning numbers. The firefighters always recorded the winning numbers on the chalkboard in the day room, so when he came back from the call, he looked at his ticket and the numbers on the chalkboard and thought he had won. He proceeded to tell everyone of his good fortune, even calling his family and friends and letting them know he had won. The firefighters let the charade go on too long. Since he was old enough to retire, he contemplated retirement and living high off his huge lotto winnings. Finally, after much regret, they told him what they had done, how they had falsified his lotto ticket. He was so angry that he never came back to work; he retired. Agitation carried too far, as in this case, was totally unacceptable. There is a limit to how much agitation should sting. Once that limit is exceeded to the point of damaging relationships, permanently as in this case, it should be reined in. Preserving relationships is vital.

CHAPTER 13

Trapped

The shift at the firehouse was rather uneventful so far. I relieved the firefighter who worked my position on the fire engine and started to check the equipment. All equipment must work when we need it, so inspection of equipment was required.

I put my bunker gear in my jump seat, grabbed a helmet, and began checking my breathing apparatus. I put an anti-fogging agent on my mask and charged the mask to see if it had leaks or other problems. It must work when I need it. In the 1980s, we used Scott air packs. These backpacks consisted of a steel bottle, with a maximum of thirty minutes of air, if breathing normally. An exhausted firefighter breathing heavily, or a scared firefighter lost in the smoke in the interior of a structure, could easily deplete his tank in fifteen minutes. The mask covered the face creating a seal that kept the clean air in and the smoke out. While working inside under super-heated conditions, the mask would always begin to fill up with facial sweat. After fifteen minutes in a high-heat environment, it was not unusual to have facial sweat pool in the mask and slosh back and forth just beneath the nose. First-timers in those conditions would typically ask where all the water in their mask was coming from?

In the kitchen, the officer had been standing over a pot of pinto beans, slowly stirring the beans as the ashes from the cigarette in his mouth fell into the pot–seasoning dinner. Nobody cared or complained, we were all just thankful he was cooking supper for the boys.

In the 1980s, many of the firefighters who smoked cigarettes were active firefighters before the advent of the breathing apparatus. In earlier days, it was a badge of honor if a firefighter could take a lot of smoke. Some could take a tremendous amount of smoke and still get the job done. They learned to "sip" smoke. Breathing with their chin right above a fog nozzle set at full fog would help to breathe smoke without choking, hacking, or coughing as much. Damp smoke was easier to breathe. Fog nozzles also created a lot of steam. The steam mixed with smoke was easier to breathe, but the steam displaced oxygen, creating a bit of a complication.

After extinguishing a structure fire, it would be necessary to pull ceilings and strip walls to find hidden hot spots. It was hot, grueling, physical work but necessary to make sure there would be no rekindle. The smoke would still be heavy in the initial stages of an extinguished fire, but locating a firefighter working inside was made easier by looking for the glow of his cigarette.

Why was there such a disregard for their own health? I have a few anecdotal theories, but nothing more. When entering the fire service, applicants are given extra points on their written scores for being a military veteran. Consequently, a large number of veterans served in the fire department. Some of these veterans served in combat zones where waking up the following day was a gift. Retirement was not high on the list of things they looked forward to; basic survival took precedence. This mentality carried over to their work in the fire service. A focus on the short term, not giving much thought to longevity, permeated their thought processes.

The other theory I had was their desire for recognition from their peers. Not only being good at firefighting, but being the best "smoke eater" at their respective fire houses was the pinnacle of success. The pride in a job well done kept their heads held high, even if their lungs were black. The effects of smoke would be evident even after the advent of the breathing apparatus. It permeated the nose, ears, and skin. I would take a shower during and after my shift and my wife would say that I still smelled like a barbeque pit. Cotton swabs in my ears and paper tissue from my nose would be black after use. The harmful effect of smoke slowly destroyed firefighters' health.

It was after supper and dark. We locked the exterior doors to the station to prevent theft. There is an emergency buzzer on the outside wall of the firehouse that people could ring if they had an emergency. No sooner had we locked up the station than the alarm went off for a structure fire in the courts. We arrived on the scene to find a three-bedroom ground floor apartment with the living room fully involved in fire. Because it was on the ground floor a heavy metal mesh covered all the windows to prevent break-ins and theft. We pulled a preconnect line and approached the building. A woman's voice could be heard screaming from a back room. She was trapped by the fire in the living room. My officer was in front of me, already trying to knock down the flames enough so that we could get in and rescue. He assigned me and Shade to get inside for search and rescue. Shade and I turned on our breathing apparatus and entered the structure. We crawled across the living room floor and made our way toward the back of the house. Before we could get to the hallway, Shade tapped me and signaled mask trouble; he had to exit. I turned into the first bedroom and continued searching. To my surprise there was an unconscious toddler, maybe a one year old, lying on his back on the floor in the middle of the room. He was not breathing.

I scooped him up and found the closest window. The truck men removed the wire mesh and I passed him out the window to the driver of our fire engine. The driver started immediate mouth-to-mouth resuscitation. I dropped back to the floor and continued my search. I seemed to be operating at twice the normal speed, but still too slow. The mental energy required to focus seemed to approach overload. I knew that each breath of dense smoke the trapped woman inhaled lessened her chance of survival.

This rescue operation was different from the onset. The initial perceived urgency created by the screams of the trapped woman put me on high alert–both mentally and physically. I'm familiar with adrenaline surge, but this was a new level, a higher gear that I wasn't aware existed. Losing my rescue partner to equipment failure had removed the possibility of routine from this rescue operation. Finding an unconscious toddler not breathing was totally unexpected. This discovery caused my mind to wonder how many more kids needing rescue might be in other rooms I had not searched yet. This was a daunting concern.

The smoke was still too heavy, visibility was impossible except for a space from the level of the floor up to about six inches. I crawled to the hallway, found the next bedroom, and crawled in. The lady who was trapped and screaming was now unconscious, lying on her back on the floor. She was too big for me to carry, so I set her up in a sitting position on the floor and grabbed her around the torso under her arms. She wore a silky nightgown which made it difficult to get a good grip to lift her. I was already tired, now seemingly alone, and the unconscious woman was heavy. Moving an unconscious person is like moving dead weight. If she weighed two hundred pounds, that was the carry weight. There was no help moving her, I really needed Shade.

Simply moving her was one thing. Moving her to safety intensified the effort required considerably. I estimated her weight at about two hundred pounds, outweighing me by roughly twenty-five pounds. After I got her in the sitting position with my arms around her torso, I had to lift her high enough to keep her butt from dragging on the burned debris on the floor. To lift her too high would lift her head too close to the heat emanating from the ceiling, so I had to hold her in my arms while I assumed a seated position–but without a chair. Moving her would involve duck walking backwards in a semi-squatting position. Holding two hundred pounds of silky, slippery, unconscious weight in front of me while I squatty stepped backwards pushed my limits with each step.

The weight of my own gear, which felt like being wrapped in four blankets, plus the forty-five-pound steel air tank, weighed me down. The energy-draining, elevated temperature inside the fire structure exacerbated my problem. I slowly, painfully, dragged her toward the bedroom exit door into the hallway. My legs burned intensely, not from the heat, but from muscle fatigue. I struggled to get her to what I thought was the living room, but I still could not see anything in the dense, black smoke. I was lost and alone with the clock running on her oxygen deficit. I couldn't find the exit door to get outside; no visibility existed in the heavy smoke.

After I became disoriented in the main room, with no clue which way led outside, my mental composure and physical reserves dwindled exponentially. I fought the negativity in my own mind that was telling me that I was too tired to continue; to just leave her, go get help, and come back in. I told myself that if I left her, my second attempt at rescue would surely be a body recovery. We continued on, together.

I played my last card, lifted my mask and called for my officer in the engulfing smoke. It was a desperation play, but it paid off. Although I couldn't see him, I knew he was there; he was always there, working inside every burning structure that had even the remotest possibility of gaining entry. He would die trying to pull off a successful rescue, apparently, I would too. We never talked about the bond we had, but we both were aware of it. I've come to realize over the years that we could both push the limits of courage further, to the edge of catastrophic failure, while working with each other. We had a safety net in each other that others were not aware of. A relationship of trust, possibly like a Navy Seal Tactical Team, vowing never to leave one another behind.

My officer appeared and took hold of the unconscious victim's legs to lift them off the floor, allowing me to walk forward instead of backward, saving much time. He guided us to the exit door. We made it outside, carried her to the front yard, and laid her on the ground. Paramedics were on the scene now; it was now their turn to work the rescue.

I pulled my mask off and fell to the ground. My legs had finally given out once we had her safely outside. My energy reserves were depleted. I laid on the ground outside, desperately trying to get more fresh air into my lungs. I remembered seeing a firefighter I didn't know leaning over me on one knee asking if I was okay. This was the first time in memory I had pushed the limits of my physical capabilities beyond what I thought possible–beyond my own perceived limitations.

I had been physically and mentally exhausted before, but this was something different. I had gone beyond the screaming in my head telling me that it was time to slow down a notch, pace myself, and focus more on self preservation. The trapped woman screaming from the back of the house when we pulled up set the tone. A woman startled by a mouse screams with a startled shriek. A woman traumatized by the thought of imminent death screams with every fiber of her being, at the top of her lungs, loud and unceasing. It was the first time I heard the fear-of-death scream–a sound I will never forget.

Finding the woman who had been screaming, now unconscious in another room, had caused me to desperately miss my rescue partner, Shade. Working with a rescue partner, as opposed to alone, brings a sense of comfort and control to an otherwise seemingly uncontrollable situation.

The little toddler and the mother were successfully resuscitated. Shade kept apologizing to me about his equipment failure. I get it. You can do everything to maintain your equipment but sometimes things break. Overall, it was a good night. Two good saves, nobody hurt. Our officer bought us all Gatorades on the ride home over the bridge. We were a damn good crew.

Being able to rely on your partners when chaos descends is everything. It's one thing to get through a dangerous shift once or twice without help from your brothers, but it is virtually impossible to do it for years. You need them and they need you. It's a symbiotic relationship where both parties not only benefit, but need one another for survival.

CHAPTER 14

The Abyss into Hell

We rolled out on a fire in the downtown area. It was nighttime, and an arsonist had torched a classic-car museum. We could still get inside the structure, even though it was well involved with fire. My officer called for a big line with a "big dick," which is slang for a playpipe nozzle. This hose configuration flows massive amounts of water but is hard to move around and has serious back pressure. Our officer always joked about water pressures. He despised a limp hose line with weak pressure. He always said to keep increasing the pressure until he's on his tiptoes, then back it off ten psi.

We gained entry through doors on the first floor and tried to get up the stairs to the mezzanine landing. The mezzanine was over the fire, with the cars burning underneath us, but an ideal location for our line. There was limited visibility in the thick, black smoke, so we donned our masks and turned on our air. The heavy fire on the showroom floor was intensifying, so we tried to muscle the big line up the stairs to the mezzanine loft over the fire. It was hard to manipulate the big line into position because it had already been pressurized, so the added weight of the water in the line posed a difficult struggle as we tried to reach the landing. The landing was scorching hot being above the fire, but we settled into the task of trying to tie off the hose line with rope hose tools. These tools were short ropes looped on metal hooks used to tie off big lines to support the line and handle the back pressure during long, drawn-out fire engagements.

I started to position myself on the other side of my officer to finish tying off the line when he threw his arm across my chest and grabbed my bunker coat. I moved my head to try to see his face in his mask, but I couldn't see it in the heavy smoke. I backed up and held my position behind him. After what seemed like a long time my low-air alarm sounded, so I signaled my officer that I was heading out to change out air bottles. I got a new bottle and went back in. Visibility was much better, we could see shapes now, just not in detail. I took my position behind my officer. He signaled to me and pointed to the floor on which we were squatting. Directly in front of him was a three-foot-diameter hole burned in the floor. Had he not grabbed me earlier, I would have fallen through the hole into the burning inferno on the first floor. He saved my life that evening.

I drove home after my shift, walked in the front door, and my wife asked me how my shift went. I replied, "Fine," and went to bed where the red, burning, itching eyes received cure from a black, drooling, stupor for the next four hours.

CHAPTER 15

PTSD Begins with Hurt Kids

PTSD Begins with Hurt Kids

P TSD Begins with Hurt Kids
It was about 10:00 a.m., twenty-two hours into a twenty-four-hour shift. We had started to clean up the firehouse to get ready for relief time when a call came in for a fire close to the firehouse. It was a shack of a house with a chain-link fence around the small front yard. It was a hot day already, and not even noon yet. We pulled up in front of the house and saw a little boy, maybe six years old, standing in the front yard screaming. The front-porch area of the house was still burning, so we attended to the fire on the porch and at the same time rendered aid to the little boy.

He had thick black hair and dark brown skin. His little face was wearing his pain. He was standing, wearing a little pair of white underwear and no other clothes. At first, I thought he had pale white socks on, but on closer observation it was not socks at all, but he was burned so badly that the skin around his lower legs had detached from his legs and was now bagging around his ankles like loose- fitting socks. I continued hosing him off with a garden hose in the front yard while he screamed in my ear until the ambulance arrived. While trying to cool off his burns with the water from the garden hose, I noticed the extent of his burns. Arms, legs, buttocks, back, and chest. All he could do was continue to cry with a look on his face that begged me to help him.

We loaded him in the ambulance for transport to the burn- center hospital. The porch fire was out but still smelled like gasoline. He had been playing with a toy truck on the front porch. His father was at work so the unsupervised little boy had taken a gas can from the porch, unscrewed the cap on the gas can, and proceeded to gas up his toy truck. In the process of refueling his truck, he spilled gas all over the porch. The pilot light from the gas hot-water heater in the corner of the porch ignited the spilled gasoline. His burns were so severe that he died later in the hospital.

Emergency calls involving little children, especially where the child is hurt badly or killed, seem never to leave a first responder's consciousness. Combat soldiers, firefighters, police, paramedics, emergency-care nurses and doctors, all mentally carry these emergencies that replay in their minds for years. Recalling every detail of the run, it plays in the consciousness while awake through triggers, and while sleeping through nightmares, that come and go and repeat throughout the years. First responders, haunted by the fact that maybe something could have been done to alter the outcome in a favorable way, continue to mentally process the emergency over and over in their minds. Any sanity that can be had comes through focusing on the thought that you did everything you could possibly do to help or save the victim. Hope must replace doubt to have any chance of mental health going forward. This struggle is exacerbated by the mental gymnastics required to prepare for the next emergency call when the previous call has not been fully processed. This compounding effect changed me.

We pulled up in front of the firehouse after we made an emergency run. A car was blocking the ramp that we must use to get the fire engine back in position in the bay for our next emergency. The ambulance parked on the back ramp of the firehouse in the same bay that the fire engine uses, so the fire engine could only back in instead of pulling in forward.

The car parked on the street, blocking our path, was waiting to get free cheese and other food staples from the community-outreach building next door to the firehouse. The driver of the car saw us waiting to pull back into the firehouse, so he started his engine and began to move slowly forward. I was still seated on the fire engine watching him move forward when I saw the back part of his car rise about six inches off the roadway. Knowing there was no bump in the roadway in front of the ramp, I jumped off the fire engine, yelled at the driver and waved my arms–frantically trying to get his attention. He stopped. I got close enough to see the bump, which wasn't a bump in the roadway, but a small toddler; the rear tire rested in the middle of the child's back. I calmly told the driver not to move the car another inch because there was a small child trapped under his rear tire. Had he continued forward one more foot his wheel would have rolled over the toddler's head.

The driver of the car had been sitting in the car with the driver's door open while he waited. The car was a two-door, so the little child had managed to squeeze out of the car from the back seat, without the driver knowing. After being safely extricated and transported by ambulance, we learned that the child suffered internal injuries, but we were thankful for another save. This could have easily gone the other way.

CHAPTER 16

Structure-Fire Life

Interior firefighting has become a lost art. In the 1980s, firefighting was quite different than it is today. In poor neighborhoods many people did not have insurance on their houses or home furnishings. If their homes caught fire and burned to the ground, they lost their homes and all of their possessions. No insurance company would be issuing a reimbursement check for their loss. Consequently, if a fire erupted in a poor person's home, it was not unusual to find the homeowner with a garden hose inside the house or attic, feverishly spraying water trying to save their possessions while choking on heavy smoke.

In extreme cases, poverty could remove any semblance of normality from life. I once saw heavy smoke pouring from a bedroom window of a house in our fire-district neighborhood. Upon investigation, we found a woman in the smoke-filled bedroom. She was cooking meat in the bedroom on a large, outdoor barbecue grill. Tears ran from her eyes, and snot ran down her face as she was tending to the smoking meat. Periodically she was putting a towel up to her mouth to help her breath without coughing. I asked her what she was doing cooking meat in the bedroom. She looked at me with a tortured, exasperated look on her face and replied through fits of coughing, "If I bobby q [sic] outside, they steals [sic] my meat."

Structural firefighting today has evolved into a precise, tactical procedure involving set maneuvers for different scenarios. The wheels on the fire engine do not move until each firefighter is totally bunkered out, wearing all their protective gear and seatbelted in. In most cases, the first-arriving fire-engine officer assumes command of the scene until a chief officer arrives. If an urgent rescue is needed, the first arriving officer could pass command of the scene via radio and switch to rescue mode. All this response preparation costs precious time.

In the 1980s, it was a high-stakes game of racing to the scene. The driver of the fire engine would take off as soon as the crew jumped on–sometimes while the crew was jumping on. Occasionally a rookie wouldn't get on in time to ride to the fire and would be reprimanded when the officer got back to the firehouse. No seat belts were used, and if the fire was close to the firehouse, it was not unusual for the crew to be half dressed while trying to pull hose lines. Whatever it took to beat the other fire engines responding to the scene, that's what was done. Arrival at the scene involved a head knowledge of what needed to be done and was not based on a set tactical scenario.

If the second fire-engine crew to arrive saw hose lines leading inside the structure, it was an interior attack. If heavy fire precluded an interior attack, firefighters laid big lines to supply aerial ladder trucks while they sprayed water from the exterior.

There has been a paradigm shift in fire responses and structural firefighting in the last forty years. The current fire responses and tactics have shifted to a safety focus to protect firefighters at all costs, understandably so. Fair enough, people today are more heavily insured, with losses covered by insurance. Fire chiefs at the scene of commercial structures are not willing to risk firefighter safety in marginal structure fires, where sending them inside the structure may result in injury or death. The commercial buildings are insured; no problem if they burn down. Cities are not willing to assume the liability costs of firefighter injuries and vehicle damage possibly incurred by rushing to the scene as well.

The problem with the modern process occurs when slow response times interfere with timely rescues. The extra minute it may take to get out of the fire station may be the difference between a successful rescue or a body recovery. Firefighters haven't changed. Firefighters still want to do the job to the best of their abilities, it's the restrictions placed on them by the cities that hamper them. Emergency rescue has always been a game of seconds where time is a luxury but not always available.

I worked a fire as a driver engineer one night where the fire was so close to the firehouse that there were no other fire engines arriving for quite a while. I connected to a fire hydrant close to the fire, which was burning an old abandoned movie theater close to downtown, while the attack crew took a preconnect into the theater. The fire officer began an interior attack in combination with search and rescue. It was late at night, so the chance of homeless vagrants sleeping inside the theater was strong, especially in the neighborhood close to the firehouse. My regular officer was on vacation, so I was handling the pump pressures while the regular driver was in the active-officer position. He had no time to put his breathing apparatus on, so he took a line and went inside without his mask or air tank. After quite a while the chief arrived and took command of the scene from the exterior. No other fire engines had arrived yet, so no backup was available for my officer and the other firefighter.

The two of them finally emerged from the theater. The chief saw them come out coughing and spitting with snot rolling down their faces. He yelled at them to get back inside until more help arrived.

They both went back inside the burning theater, until help finally arrived.

After the fire was out, I was talking to the acting officer on my crew and the other firefighter. They were both sick, having taken a snout full of smoke. We refer to this type of structure fire fought with no breathing apparatus as a "snot slinger." I thought about how courage and perseverance is a necessary character attribute for an effective interior firefighter. Respect amongst your peers, no matter what your rank, is of greatest value to any firefighter throughout his career. This respect is only gained through courage and a persevering attitude. Quitting was never an option.

The responding chief who sent my acting officer back inside the structure with no breathing apparatus, happened to be his father. It appeared that a positive generational legacy was the next most important thing behind courage and perseverance.

It was 3:00 am. The alarm in the firehouse sounds for a multiple-alarm structure fire. We rolled out of the bunks and headed toward the poles to slide down to the first floor and board the fire engine. I had been sleeping in a position that cut off circulation to one of my arms. I let two firefighters slide the pole ahead of me while trying to get some feeling in my arm. Time's up! I slid the pole with one dead arm.

The fire advanced to another alarm while we were still rolling. It turned out to be a large furniture warehouse, with showrooms displaying living and bedroom settings so eager buyers would be enticed to buy, especially with the sixty-month, easy-payment plans.

We were the second-arriving fire engine. The warehouse was roaring with fire shooting through the roof thirty feet above the structure. The tilt-wall construction of the walls was starting to separate at one of the corners at the top–gapping two feet at the top edge. We laid two lines from the aerial truck positioned near the side of the building and caught the nearest fire hydrant. The aerial truck could pour 1500 gpm on the fire from an elevated nozzle. The roof was already partially collapsed, so the water from the aerial nozzle would be able to penetrate the structure effectively, especially where the collapsed portion of the roof did not impede the aerial streams.

Now we waited, letting the aerial platforms do their job. Interior firefighting was not possible until the aerial truck's elevated nozzle streams could get ahead of the fire. Once the main body of fire could be extinguished enough to let fire crews inside, the elevated streams were shut down. The interior crew would finish extinguishing the remaining fire and search for bodies.

We laid dry leader lines from the nearest fire engine, got them in position, and waited for the order to go inside the burning structure. The chief gave the order. We charged our lines with water and started making our way inside the building. It was hot, but not unbearable. Visibility was poor, even with the partial roof collapse. We moved slowly, trying not to miss any bodies or hidden fire, as we got to the middle of the building. Visibility was still only about three feet in a crouched position, but it was getting better instead of worse.

Suddenly, without warning, I heard the loudest explosion I've ever heard. The concrete floor under our feet shook violently as the interior crew searched for the origin of the explosion. We kept moving forward through the building toward where the sound came from. Thirty more feet forward and we hit a concrete step, about a foot and a half tall that appeared to be another floor elevation. We stepped up on the new concrete floor and continued forward, dragging our line. After walking another twenty feet forward the smoke was gone, the air was clear, and we were all standing outside. It was then we realized that the deafening explosion we heard was the exterior wall collapsing and falling outward, away from the building. What we thought was another floor elevation was the fallen exterior wall. The 40-foot-tall exterior wall was now a seventy-five-foot-long flat concrete patio.

The fire had gone to a fourth-alarm fire. We spent all night at the scene and were the last fire company to leave the scene the following morning. We backed into the firehouse and started cleaning our tools and other equipment, washed and hung the dirty fire hose to dry, and began cleaning the firehouse for the oncoming shift, which relieved us at noon. Driving home dead tired, my mind kept flashing back to the falling-wall incident. Had the wall fallen inward on the firefighters instead of outward, it would have been instant death for our crew. Concrete measuring a foot and a half thick would have crushed all of us, killing us instantly.

Firefighters get killed through no fault of their own; it is the nature of the work. The willingness to do the job–to push the limits of their own safety to carry out a rescue or extinguishment under extreme duress–is what separates firefighters from others not so willing to stretch the limits.

Dissecting my thoughts further, I began pondering why the line between death and life appears so random. *Why do some survive and others, equally as capable, die?* Witnessing some form of death almost every shift makes me realize how thankful I am just to live another day. Things that used to be important to me are no longer important. My priorities in life are shifting, I can feel it, almost daily. Each time an experience ends with the thought, "Wow, that was close," the priorities in life shift. The question remains: *Why do firefighters, or any rescue workers for that matter, choose this for a career?* Besides the obvious reason of having a great dental plan, it's a valid question–one that I have pondered many times myself. There's one thing for sure: Delivering hope to someone on possibly the worst day of their lives, helping them to live another day, or to make their lives just a little bit more tolerable–less of a living hell–makes the work worthwhile. I am not paranoid or afraid to die, I just now realize that growing old is measured not by the number of years you live, but by the number of days. Some shifts become the number of minutes or seconds you survive if lost in a burning structure and run out of air or are involved in a building collapse.

Death to me, since seeing the apparition, is nothing but a transition into another reality. A reality that awaits us all, when we take our last breath, we merely begin another adventure. Wow, that was close.

CHAPTER 17

Too Late

Beautifully restored homes on the edge of downtown sat like proud aristocrats on a manicured, tree-lined street–standing stately in rows, proudly negating the destructive effect of time. Magnificent, nineteenth–century architecture graced the exteriors and interiors of these timeless homes. Restorations that preserved original features such as carriage steps, for stepping out of horse drawn carriages, still adorned the sidewalks by the street. Hitching posts on which to tie horses remained on some of these stately manors. These homes resided in a historic district of the city. Nothing was allowed to be changed from the original architectural plans. Mostly wood frame, these three-story homes with huge attic spaces and root cellars were like proud ladies, gracefully beautifying the neighborhood, undisturbed by time, until...

It was 4:00 am on a cold winter morning. The alarm sounded for a structure fire. The fire was in the historic district, only a short distance from our response district. We rolled out and arrived on the scene quickly, but we were still not first in; two other fire engines were already on scene. The fire has grown exponentially due to the hundred-year-old, now-dry wood used to construct them, so to get inside and attempt a rescue was impossible. We prepared hose lines for an exterior attack, hoping we could knock the flames down enough to keep the fire from spreading to adjacent structures. Another crew member and I were trying to position a big line into the back yard before charging it with water. We got to the backyard fence and tried to throw the dry hose line over it. The fence was partially wood with a metallic angle iron frame. My partner threw the two-and-a-half inch diameter hose, it looped around the iron railing and swung back toward him, striking him in the mouth with the steel hose coupling. The coupling left a respectable gash to his lower lip. It didn't look good. He wiped the blood with his dirty glove and kept working.

We finally got the fire knocked down enough to get inside, but it took too long. Any chance of a live rescue was gone. We worked our way to the second floor and positioned our line to flood the interior. There was nothing to save but our reputation for not having any rekindles. No one wants to go back to the scene twelve hours later to put the fire out all over again. Visibility was still poor inside, but it was not unbearably hot. Finally, the smoke dissipated enough to see. We were in what appeared to be a hallway, but it was burned away to the point that it did not resemble a hallway anymore. Burned debris on the floor was about six inches deep. I had been kneeling for quite some time, but now that the smoke was clearing, I could see the shape of a body on the floor two feet from my right leg. After extinguishment, a total of seven bodies were recovered from the fire.

The time of this late-night fire, coupled with the rapid combustion characteristics of the old, dry wood, caught the residents unaware and unable to escape. Combined with the firefighter's inability to perform rescue due to the advanced stage of the fire, this tragic fire resulted in the worst possible loss of life—no survivors. We spent the remainder of the shift on scene flooding the structure and watching the sun rise in the sky. My partner went to the hospital and got his lip stitched up. We headed to our firehouse, cleaned up the equipment and the firehouse, and went home. On the majestic, historic street, one of the proud ladies was now missing, taking with her seven people who will never see another sunrise. Rough shift.

CHAPTER 18

No Such Thing as a Routine Fire

Structural firefighting could be learned through experience, but even the most learned, experienced firefighters know that in this business, nothing is routine. Things change instantaneously. Knowing the fundamentals, combined with regular training and a healthy dose of courage can help, but in no way could guarantee, a successful outcome on every run. Without making any mistakes, other than signing on to be a firefighter, one can quickly find oneself in a tragedy in the making.

Midafternoon, on a hot summer day, we arrived at a house fire with flames that were originating from the rear of the house. Textbook firefighting called for an interior attack from the unburned side of the house, which in this case, would be the street side. We laid a preconnect line and approached the front of the structure. Heavy, black smoke billowed out the front door and windows; we crouched to a crawl and entered the front door. Usually when visibility was limited because of heavy smoke, at least it would be possible to have some visibility near the floor, but not always.

On this day, visibility was near zero. I was on the nozzle; another member of the crew pulled line behind me as we inched across the floor. I hadn't opened the nozzle at all. We were still searching for the main body of fire; still not visible. Inching across the floor slowly by feel, we went from our entry point at the front door to the opposing wall, about fifteen to twenty feet from our entry. This could have been the living room. We felt our way down the wall until we could reach an opening that might lead us to the back of the house. We came to an opening. It was a doorway. We crawled through into the second room, bumping into wooden chair legs as we dragged the hoseline forward. Throwing the chairs to the side, we then crawled directly under a kitchen or dining room table, still not sure which, and continued on our way. It was at this point that it started to get hot.

I tried scanning the room but could see nothing until I looked directly overhead toward the ceiling. An orange glow had lit up the ceiling above our heads, the source of the increased heat. The orange glow was right above us in every direction. It had somehow gotten in behind us, which had removed the word "routine" from this fire. Lying on the floor, I put the nozzle on full fog and aimed it at the ceiling. Fire was now between our entry point into the house and where we were now lying on the floor. We were faced with the choice of abandoning our nozzle and trying to escape by following our own line back out the way we came, or trying to bend our charged line, keeping the nozzle. This would involve making it back through the two doorways we had just crawled through without kneeling or standing. To kneel or stand would have been impossible with the amount of fire above our heads. Neither was a good option. I said a silent 911 prayer consisting of three words, "Lord, help us!"

Before having a second to weigh either option, the line we held began moving back toward the direction from which we came. At this point, I kept the nozzle on full fog directed at the ceiling, and we held tightly onto the line while it was being pulled toward the door we entered. We held on to the hose line the whole time until we found ourselves safely outside on the porch where we started.

The third firefighter on our crew who had helped position our line before we entered the house, was getting ready to mask up and follow the line inside to help me and the other crewmember when he noticed a serious danger. It was when he was standing on the porch readying himself for entry that he noticed not just heavy smoke, but fire exiting the doorway, and our hose line going into the house directly under the fire. He realized we were in trouble, so he started manually pulling the line out of the structure, hoping we were still holding on to the business end of the hose.

We continued with extinguishment from a different entry point, finally extinguishing the fire. It was then we realized that the front room we had started our initial attack in had not one, but two doorways, on the far wall that we had bumped into. Fire had come through the other doorway, not the doorway leading to the kitchen that we had crawled through, and had worked its way around the front room, thereby getting behind us and cutting off our exit. We had inadvertently violated a fundamental of structural firefighting: Never let the fire get behind you.

Had it not been for the heads-up thinking of the third crew member, we might have been severely burned in this routine fire. The lesson for me that day was that nothing was routine in firefighting. There were too many variables in emergency work that would not allow for any assumption of routine, ever.

This fire was one of a series of fires over the course of my firefighting career that reinforced the transience of life. I learned never to assume tomorrow will come. As a child, waiting for Christmas to come, I wanted the days to pass quickly. They didn't. Now, after experiencing many days that could have easily resulted in my own funeral, I try to enjoy every day, if possible, and never get in a hurry for things to be over. I know it may be cliché, but living in the moment became my mantra. To count on tomorrow coming is a fool's game. We have no clue how long we will be on this Earth. Jesus teaches this in a parable He spoke to His listeners.

[16] And he told them a parable, saying, "The land of a rich man produced plentifully, [17] and he thought to himself, 'What shall I do, for I have nowhere to store my crops?' [18] And he said, 'I will do this: I will tear down my barns and build larger ones, and there I will store all my grain and my goods. [19] And I will say to my soul, "Soul, you have ample goods laid up for many years; relax, eat, drink, be merry."' [20] But God said to him, 'Fool! This night your soul is required of you, and the things you have prepared, whose will they be?' (Luke 12.16-20).

Near-death experiences serve a vital function in transforming one's thought processes to be fully aware that life can end at any time. The more near-death experiences one has, the more transformative change can occur. Saying, "Wow, that was close," a number of times causes a mental release on the tight grip of self preservation. Not to be cavalier, or careless, but a definite release occurs–one that speaks to the soul. A message that life continues on Earth, until it doesn't. And that it has an end, and no one knows when that day is. The transformation begins, then progressively increases with each close call until a total transformation occurs. Death is not the worst thing. There are many things worse than death.

My father, who had lived through the horrors of World War II as an Army combat soldier for five years, knew all about the transience of life. When he was old he used to tell me to try to enjoy the little things in life as you travel this road. He would say to sit in the shade and enjoy a sweet, juicy orange. Savor the flavor, unhurriedly. It costs nothing, except the price of the orange, but it is rewarding in true satisfaction. All the money in the world may not buy a better experience of peaceful bliss. Ask a person in stage- four terminal cancer what is important in life. Use the answers as a valid starting point toward a path to a life well lived.

CHAPTER 19

Street-Paramedic Life

Fire department paramedics in large metro cities have extremely difficult, and one of the most rewarding, jobs. After several years working as a firefighter, I became eligible to take a written exam to be promoted to the next rank. The exam is one hundred questions, multiple choice, timed and written. All passing grades are listed in order of highest score to lowest passing score, combined with the candidate's longevity up to ten years.

Promotions are made when a firefighter retires, which creates a vacancy. These vacant positions need to be filled. The vacancy in my case would normally be for a Fire Engineer, who is the driver and pump operator on a fire engine or truck. Some candidates will be set aside to become students in the next paramedic class. The paramedic class is a forty-hour week of in-class instruction for six months, combined with hospital rotations and ambulance ride outs. After six months, the student graduates, then reports for duty on an ambulance, full–time at one of the firehouses.

While studying to get promoted and go to paramedic training, I studied the required promotional study books for six months prior to taking the exam and scored a seventy, second from the bottom on the eligibility list. I came home and told my wife my score. After having watched me study for six months, she replied, "No really, tell me what you really made."

The next year I scored second from the top of the list and ended up in the next paramedic class. After six months I graduated and was assigned to the same working firehouse in which I had been a firefighter, only now I was working as a paramedic on the ambulance with no fire duty. A slow shift on the ambulance at my current station was ten emergency calls per twenty-four-hour shift. The record number of calls I made from that firehouse in one shift was twenty-three. Average calls per shift were about fifteen. Paramedics assigned to my firehouse would say a good shift is not determined by the total calls per shift, but the number of calls you make after midnight.

Shift change was 7:00 am, so from 4:00 am to 7:00 am was the time when most of the ambulance tires would be damaged from hitting curbs. Sleep deprived paramedics, having driven patients to the hospitals for the last twenty-one hours, could drive erratically from sheer exhaustion and sleep deprivation.

I used to get off work at 7:00 am and get in my pickup truck to drive home while half asleep. Not a good strategy. I remember how I got angry at other people sitting in traffic while on my way home from work, people I didn't even know. Looking at their fresh, rested faces, driving their cars to work with their steamy cup of coffee in their hand, I would be mad at them for no reason. I knew it was sleep deprivation and exhaustion that caused my unwarranted anger, but it annoyed me.

The hood of my truck was the same color as the hood on the ambulance, so my sleep deprivation deceived me quite often. Looking through my windshield on my pickup truck looked exactly like looking through the windshield of the ambulance. Even though I was off duty, I approached red lights at intersections, and instead of stopping as I should, I slowed my pickup truck to make sure it was clear before proceeding through the intersections and cruised right through the intersection while the light was still red. I needed to sell my truck or paint it a different color.

The neighborhood where I worked was probably a lot like most poverty-stricken neighborhoods in major cities throughout the U.S.: rampant drugs and crime, never enough of what people really needed to survive and thrive, yet an abundance of hardship and misery. Subsidized housing dominated, with women and children living off government subsidies to stay alive. In the midst of all this agony, anguish, and despair, there remained an underlying sense of hope for a better day among many of the residents. These hopeful residents gave me hope. Were it not for them, I would have struggled to maintain hope myself. It was easy to develop an attitude of despair and hopelessness with a seemingly never-ending supply of overdoses, gunshot wounds, stabbings, cuttings, and innocent children caught in the fray, for no other reason than they were growing up in the neighborhood.

Rendering medical treatment in the neighborhood required completing the patient form and asking basic questions. It was not uncommon to ask a man in the neighborhood what his address was, and he would look at you with a blank stare. It was always necessary to ask a man where they "stayed" to get a suitable answer. When questioning bystanders about a medical patient, they would sometimes say that the patient "fell out." This means that the patient lost consciousness. Many rookie paramedics have responded with the question, "They fell out of what?"

Once the ambulance pulled into the projects—or courts, during daylight hours, the paramedics became the neighborhood doctor making house calls. While treating someone having a seizure or a sick person, little children would come to the apartment and ask you if you would come to their house too because someone was hurt or injured in their house. I've treated four separate emergencies on one assigned call before being able to leave the neighborhood.

Many times, if the call was for a diabetic emergency, the patient would come to the ambulance because they were homeless. Once in the ambulance, the paramedic would typically start an IV on the patient and administer a vial of D50 to get the sugar level up. Once the sugar level was normalized and preparations made for hospital transport, the patient would pull the IV out of his arm and jump out of the ambulance before it started moving. The fake name and information on the patient form guaranteed there would be no bill to pay.

Drug users were just the opposite. When heavy drug users sustained a gunshot or stab wound, they would find the ambulance and jump in if able to do so. Addicts' veins were sometimes ruined by too many illegal drug injections, so paramedics would then be faced with the near impossible task of finding a vein for IV insertion. I've seen veteran paramedics hand the IV needle to the addict to start his own IV. The addicts knew where their best veins were, and I have yet to see one miss a stick. I learned to hand them the needle on occasion as well.

When it was dark, daylight rules no longer applied. Rules of operation changed considerably. Getting a call in the projects at night was a different game. As soon as we drove into the projects, there was usually no way to find where to go. All the street signs and housing numbers were missing, now souvenirs on living room walls. There were no streetlights. The drug trade needed to operate under cover of darkness, so the dealers shot out the street lights. We always parked in the middle of the projects with the emergency lights on, but no siren. The neighbors would see the emergency lights and bring the patient to us if possible.

This was where it got tricky. If women or children came out and tried to lead us to where the patient was, it was usually safe to go to the patient. If young men wanted us to follow them to the patient, we learned it could be a trap. They may want to lead us behind a building to beat and rob us. Many times, I have told young men to bring the patient to me. Some young men were honestly trying to help, with no malevolent plans. The difficulty remained, however, of not knowing their intent, which caused decision making to err on the side of caution. Some young men would try to get paramedics away from the ambulance so they could steal the drug kit off the ambulance, and in some cases, just steal the ambulance. One ambulance was stolen and driven away while the paramedic was in the back of the ambulance treating a patient.

In another case, I was working overtime on an ambulance that wasn't the same ambulance I normally worked on. Since I was on overtime, the shift commander moved me to a different ambulance at 10:30 pm and my replacement jumped on the ambulance I had been on. At midnight, the paramedic that took my place was shot in the arm by a stray bullet while loading a patient on the stretcher in the projects.

If the call in the projects was at night, and the call was for a shooting or cutting, the patient was easy to find. As soon as we saw a crowd of fifty people standing around in one spot, the patient would be right in the middle of the crowd. I used to ask the crowd who shot the patient, or who cut him up; the silence from the crowd would be deafening. I have never gotten an answer. After about a year, as I became more seasoned, I quit asking. Often, the reason no one would say how the patient got hurt is because the shooter or the person who assaulted the patient was standing in the crowd ensuring no one talked. Talkers were likely the next victim.

We got an emergency call for a shooting in the projects and arrived on scene. A young teenager was lying in the doorway to the apartment bleeding heavily from a gunshot wound in his upper leg area. He was wearing large parachute pants, popularized by a rap singer named MC Hammer. He was in distress but conscious and had silver spray paint on his lips. He was a "spray head," or huffer as some called them. His lips were stained with silver spray paint from spraying paint into an empty soda can or other container and holding the can up to his mouth and inhaling the fumes. It gave a temporary high, altered reality for a while, and destroyed brain cells in the process.

I finished bandaging him up and went into the apartment to see if my partner needed help with any other victims. Entering the front room, I noticed the room smelled like spray paint. I looked at the woman sitting in the room; she had silver paint around her mouth as well. This woman turned out to be the mother of the teenager I just finished bandaging. The mother was unhurt, so I checked the other rooms. In the first bedroom sat an older woman in a rocking chair. She was unhurt as well, but also had silver paint around her mouth–the grandmother of the teenager I had just bandaged.

After transporting the teen to the hospital, I began to dwell on the generational addiction I had just witnessed. I empathized with the hopeless despair they must have experienced every day, with no hope of change. Three generations of addiction in one family. Life reduced to a nihilistic hopelessness that clings to them and seemingly never releases the grip of despair and misery. Subsidies for food and housing every month, but no real life. Harsh reality, living on the jagged edge, still breathing, heart still beating, but dead inside. Disillusioned and disappointed with a life reduced to yet another rendezvous with the silver-paint can. The paint is the respite, the escape from the misery of life for a little while. With spray paint, the high is fleeting, dissipating quickly, leaving behind a roaring headache. The hellish cycle continues, maybe for generations to come.

If I hadn't seen the apparition and didn't know there is more to life than what I had observed that day, it would be easy for me to fall into the emotional darkness surrounding the generational tragedy I had witnessed. How could I not? If three generations of addiction in the same family was not enough to cause one to lose total faith in humanity and the human condition, I don't know what it would take. The apparition has spared me the pain by showing me that this tragedy of life is not all there is to the story. There is much more, I've seen it.

CHAPTER 20

OB, Oh Boy!

In paramedic school, I learned to treat all types of emergencies, from traumatic injuries to medical emergencies. The exam category on which I scored the lowest was obstetrics (OB), which were emergencies related to childbirth. OB emergencies were common in poverty pockets of the city. People with no health insurance or money typically would receive limited prenatal care, so they often suffered from multiple complications related to childbirth.

Since we responded to calls in our own area, as well as any calls in the county if we were the closest ambulance, many times we responded to emergencies on the county line. Many of these emergencies were from women who were carrying full-term babies and were already in early labor. If the pregnant woman was not an American citizen, she would catch a ride to the county line, then wait for the ambulance just inside the county line to ensure that she would be taken to the county hospital. At the county hospital, she would be taken in by ambulance, would give birth, and the child would be an American citizen by birth. These newborns were typically called anchor babies, securing familial pathways to citizenship. On my first shift, my new partner asked me if I felt ok with the different types of emergencies. I replied that my weakest area was OB emergencies, so of course, we received four calls for OB emergencies on my first shift.

The first OB call was a few blocks from the firehouse. We arrived at the courts and found the eighteen-year-old, future mother in the living room surrounded by aunts, Mom, and lots of siblings. Her water had broken. My partner started checking vitals and timing contractions. I was filling out the patient form and recording a medical history. Everything was going well; she was not in much distress. I asked about her medical history so I could fill out the medical form. Instead of asking how many pregnancies she'd had, I foolishly asked if this was her first pregnancy. As soon as the question left my mouth the whole room erupted in loud laughter. My partner turned and looked at me like I had made my first rookie mistake. When the laughter finally died down to a roar, the sweet little future mama replied that it was her fourth pregnancy. She was eighteen years old; do the math.

After finishing up with the young, pregnant-woman case, we got back in service for our next emergency call. This one was also an OB call, for a woman in distress. We arrived on the scene at a house with another very young woman in labor. She was terrified, standing, looking down between her legs at two little baby legs dangling from her body. The legs were already protruding from the womb up to the mid-thigh area of the baby. We loaded her and the baby into the ambulance, instructed her to keep from pushing as much as she was able, and we took off down the road. I was in the back of the ambulance with the young woman, opening the birth canal by hand to create a tenting airway for the baby.

En route, I called the receiving hospital with my free hand, while I attended to the woman with the other. Lucky for all of us, the military trauma center three miles from our location could receive the patient with trauma surgeons on standby for our arrival. Upon arrival at the Emergency Department, we stopped the ambulance and immediately four military doctors threw open the back doors of the ambulance. They climbed in the back of the ambulance with their medical equipment and delivered the baby using forceps. The delivery maybe took two minutes and resulted in a healthy baby and healthy momma. I stood next to the ambulance while the surgeons worked. When they came out with a new mother and baby, both healthy, I wanted to pass out cigars. There was no better feeling than knowing that our efforts resulted in such a positive outcome. Knowing how bad this could have been made the outcome that much sweeter.

It was around midnight, an OB call came in a few blocks from the firehouse. We responded to the scene: an old, wooden, two-story house divided into rental rooms. Upstairs we found a very pregnant young lady, sitting up on a double bed in a studio apartment. Living quarters, bedroom, kitchen and bathroom were all in the same room. She called 911 because she felt it was close to delivery time. We checked her and explained to her that her contractions were not close enough to be taken by ambulance, that we were for medical emergencies only. She had plenty of time to have a friend or family member give her a ride to the hospital. We filled out a patient form for a non-emergency call and left.

We returned to the firehouse and within the hour, we received another emergency call for the same address. We drove back to the same apartment and went up the stairs to check on the young woman, only now she was no longer pregnant. She had delivered the baby, allegedly with the help of a midwife, who was nowhere to be found. There was blood everywhere, smeared on walls, bedding, floor, and the new mother. She seemed to be okay, still lying in bed. The baby was near the foot of the bed, still attached to the umbilical cord, with the other end of the cord lying on the linoleum floor attached to the placenta.

I gave my partner an OB kit, which is a small cardboard box containing pretty much everything one would need to complete an emergency delivery in the field. He began cutting the umbilical cord and finishing up with momma and the baby while I got the responsibility of retrieving the placenta so we could take it to the hospital for analysis. The OB kit contained a gallon-sized plastic bag used for transporting the placenta to the hospital. I assumed that putting the placenta in the plastic bag, and then the bag in the cardboard box for transport to the hospital, should be an easy task.

This was my first attempt at retrieving a placenta, and the fact that it was on the floor presented a bit of a challenge. Pretty simple though, it would seem. I attempted to pick up the placenta from the floor and quickly learned that it was an impossible task. The consistency of a placenta is much like Jello, picking up one end caused the other end to flop out of my hand, much like a Slinky™ toy. It moved around so much when I touched it, it seemed to be alive.

After the third failed attempt at lifting it off the floor, I decided to try to slide it across the floor to the closest wall using the cardboard lid of the OB kit to propel it. I cornered it between the floor and the corner wall with the cardboard lid, and gently pushed the living gelatin slowly up the wall until I could get it to belly flop into the plastic bag. Success! About this time my partner was giving me the look that said, "What in the hell are you doing, Rookie?"

We transported a healthy mother and baby, and a slightly dirty placenta, to the hospital. For me, two lessons had been learned. First, when a pregnant woman tells you she is about ready to deliver, believe her. The second, when faced with a similar set of circumstances in the future, let your partner scoop the placenta off the floor. I took some firehouse agitation for this run. Everyone had a good laugh at my expense.

The first two years of paramedic duty were hard, but I had found my niche. I loved what I was doing, and I had become good at it. The thing that gnawed on me occasionally was the nature of the job, repeatedly seeing patients on the worst day of their lives, dealing with the overwhelming reality of life, without time to cognitively process it all. When I first started writing about the apparition, I mentioned the effect the apparition was having on me. This effect was becoming glaringly apparent because I needed to know there is more to this life than our immediate physical reality. After witnessing the endless, generational hopelessness of people living in poverty in the crime-riddled, drug-infested neighborhood in which I worked, I needed the awareness of another world, existing parallel to my current reality. The apparition had provided that insight. In retrospect, I now realize the timing of the sighting was significant. Had I seen it even a few months later than I actually did, I would not have had the mental or emotional coping mechanisms in place when I needed them the most in the field. Who knows how much of a dark, empty, emotionless, robotic shell I would have become without the hope of another reality that exists outside our day-to-day world?

CHAPTER 21

Organized Religion

Several months passed; I was still learning in the Bible- study class I attended. The associate pastor approached me with the prospect of teaching an adult couples-class as the current teacher was leaving. I asked him to pray about it and I would pray about it as well, because I wasn't feeling it. The class was large, and it would be a bi-weekly commitment. I would need a teacher to teach the class every other week when I would be working my regular job.

Eventually, I agreed to teach. Another man who taught a Bible class befriended me and I began seeking him out after we finished teaching our classes. He was quite a bit older than me, and very knowledgeable in the Word. I asked him questions and he would respond with spiritual pearls of wisdom. He had a twenty-year head start on me as a Bible teacher. I respected him a lot.

As a Bible teacher, I learned many things he taught me and some things I learned through experience. One thing I learned right away was that not everyone has a hunger for the Word. Teachers know that there were those in the class that viewed spiritual truths as a sedative. As soon as the teacher had expounded on truths for about fifteen minutes their eyes began to close. The need for sleep trumped a desire for spiritual truths. I didn't judge them, maybe they were up all night with a sick kid or maybe they just got off from working the night shift. Who knows? It is said that the spoken word can only hold the attention of the hearer for about twenty minutes before minds drift to other things.

How many donuts were left in the back of the classroom? Was there any coffee left? What's for lunch? I wish the speaker would wind it down so we could go.

The retention rate of many hearers was also quite low. Honestly, it seemed many people didn't prioritize spiritual matters. Traditional religion had taken over and bumped much of spirituality to the curb. Appearances were everything in some peoples' minds, with little thought to the spiritual realm or an afterlife.

My frustration with traditional, denominational religion grew more intense. Although there were many legitimate churches with Spirit-filled pastors and leadership who preached truth, welcomed sinners, and reached the lost in their communities, there was also a seemingly equal number of churches that should have done everyone a favor and closed their doors. Having witnessed an authentic spiritual encounter, it was impossible for me to play church. The apparition had drastically changed my perception of organized denominational religion. I had developed a spiritual discernment, some call it a gift, that would allow me to spot a counterfeit quickly.

Learning the truth of the Word made it possible to recognize anything that wasn't truth. In my mind, counterfeit churches ran the full gamut, depending on the individual church and religion, from a definite cult, to following the traditions of man, to an extremely profitable business.

I don't blame many people for turning away from traditional denominational religion when at times it seemed many churches were operating a business with a cross on the roof. Another problem for counterfeit churches was that people were getting more and more intellectually savvy to deceptive business practices, and could smell a snake-oil salesman for miles. Intellectual progress for the masses seemed to cause a corrosive doubt and skepticism about almost everything until proven otherwise at a time where many pastors were being included in the same group with used-car salesmen, ambulance-chasing attorneys, and palm readers. Legitimate churches found it hard to survive in these conditions.

It turns out Jesus wasn't a big fan of religious leaders in His day either.

"Woe to you, scribes and Pharisees, hypocrites! For you are like **whitewashed** tombs, which outwardly appear beautiful, but within are full of dead people's **bones** and all uncleanness" (Matt. 23.27).

Jesus didn't mince words. Pharisees and Sadducees were the religious leaders during the time of Christ. Not much had changed in two thousand years. Many Spirit-filled church leaders are still around today, but sadly, some church leaders are nothing more than someone filling a pulpit. A church leader should have a spiritual calling, knowing at the deepest part of his soul that this was the path that God had placed him on, and many do. Some church leaders testified to running away from the call, not wanting to follow the urging of the Spirit, but later submitting, as similarly recorded in the scriptures. Jonah was called by God to minister to the people of Nineveh but initially refused and ran.

Not following the urgings of the Spirit is not novel; it's been happening to religious leaders since before Jesus walked the Earth. I've known church leaders that said they told God they wanted to preach. Hard to believe, but true. We should never confuse God's solutions to our problems with a decision that we made ourselves. I'm not sure if they're ever the same. We can't fix ourselves, as hard as we might try, until we turn our lives over to God for transformation. He provides a path of restoration for our lives. I came to know this from witnessing the apparition. I had been operating in my own small realm of awareness, not having a clue what was out there. I have since gained an insight into another world that exists parallel to my own reality. It changed me.

CHAPTER 22

Desperation

It was starting to get colder, uncomfortably cold for the many homeless people living on the street in our fire district. With the chill, comes desperation. Desperation makes people do crazy things, or maybe they're not so crazy after all when compared to what a sane person would do in a similar situation. Maybe I would do the same thing, assuming I'm sane.

Still a rookie paramedic, we got a call for a seizure patient on the edge of the downtown district. Upon arrival, we saw a woman and a man–a couple–homeless and cold. He was having what appeared to be a full-blown, grand mal seizure, complete with violent tremors, eyes rolled back in his head, and saliva foam running down his face. My partner was interviewing the woman, while I tried to keep the seizing man from injuring himself further. He was thrashing all over the place while I tried securing his head and neck area to maintain a patent, or unobstructed, airway.

My partner looked at me struggling with the man, walked over to us, grabbed the patient's shirt at the chest area and shook him, at the same time he yelled at the man in a loud, forceful tone, "Knock it off!" The man immediately stopped seizing. Later, I asked my veteran partner how he knew the man was faking the seizure? He said they are homeless and cold. They will do anything to get out of the cold and into a warm hospital with food. This answer turned out to be prophetic. We gave them plastic blankets from the ambulance and told them we could not take them to the hospital just because it's cold outside. Homeless shelters were an option, but pulling a city ambulance out of service to give them a ride to the hospital was not an option. We told them that they would have to be hurt, not just cold, for us to take them to the hospital.

As soon as we got back to the firehouse a call for a laceration came in around the same area we had treated the homeless couple. It was the same homeless couple, but now the woman had hit the man and caused a small cut on his forehead. We put a bandaid on the cut, gave them some more blankets, and told them the injury was not severe enough to warrant a ride to the hospital. We returned to the firehouse and received a third call for a laceration to the same location as the homeless couple. We called dispatch on the radio and explained that we had just left that area and treated a patient for a laceration. The dispatcher said they wanted us to go back to the scene, so we returned for the third time. Upon arrival, the man was bleeding profusely from a head wound. Blood from a deep gash was flowing from his forehead area. We asked him what happened and in a very angry tone he explained that his woman had hit him in the head with a brick. "Get in the ambulance."

Later, I pondered why some peoples' lives are so full of suffering when others seem to coast along as if in some type of fantasy land? The questions caused real soul searching; answers were few. Our choices seemed to factor into the equation, but there was more. Some people were born into incredible suffering yet rose out of it somehow. It had to be more than hard work and luck. Some of the hardest-working people I know never rose out of poverty and hardship. The hardship was sometimes transient, but mostly it lingered, occasionally it produced a hopeless nihilism as the suffering returned. Many suffered. Historically, there had been tremendous suffering in many parts of the world. The ones who made it through typically developed coping mechanisms–focusing on a better day to come, having an inner hope that positive change is on the horizon, thinking a better world is coming. A better day may never come, but at least they chose to believe it will.

Choosing hope in the face of adversity and suffering may alter the tragedy of life–with the multiplicity of unending problems and pain–not in altering the events themselves, but adjusting them enough to change our perception of the tragedies, giving us renewed strength that allows us to power through hopelessness. *Where does this hope come from? Why do some have it and others wallow in victimhood and despair?*

It may be because the One who allowed the apparition to find me and give me hope also happened to find them–fixing their sights on the pursuit of purpose in the midst of difficulty.

Why? Because God is sovereign over this messiness of life. The Creator transcends the mess. There is more to this chaotic life than we may realize. Witnessing evidence of the spiritual realm has confirmed this to me.

CHAPTER 23

Death

My paramedic job was exposing me to the reality of death almost every shift. I struggled to keep patients alive long enough to pass them off to receiving hospitals. Sometimes we were successful, in the more serious trauma or cardiac episodes, we had limited success. Being an active member of humanity, emotionally I died a little bit with each patient who passed, especially if there had been great effort on my part to try to keep them alive, or if they were children. Not that adults dying didn't affect caregivers, it's just that the kids seemed to have a greater effect. Sanity, at times, seemed to be a juggling act with continuous, nonstop, repeated exposure to death. *What did it all mean? Why did death visit the little kids? Why did death happen to anyone for that matter? Why were we even on this planet spinning in space?* All I had were questions with few answers.

I functioned in a constant state of compensatory cognitive function. Coping with my reality, compartmentalizing, not truly dealing with it. There was no time to process each successful, or unsuccessful, life-saving action. Too many medical emergencies in too short of a time frame.

To honestly assess and answer questions on whether there was something that could have been done better, or something that shouldn't have been done at all, needed to be analyzed on every hands-on attempt to save a life, but there was no time for that. Information was compartmentalized in my brain, set aside to deal with another day, as the next medical emergency would come over the radio. I am afraid that if God sat me down and answered all the questions I had and more, showed me my future and fate,it might be more than I could bear.. It's best that I did not know.

What I do know about death came from my near constant exposure to death and dying. Real-life examples, I have found, were sometimes the best teachers. Death was expected, no one escaped it. Death could come quickly, instantaneously for some, for others it was a slow, agonizing process.

Many soldiers, firefighters, paramedics, doctors, nurses, and first responders are well acquainted with death. Death could touch their lives often, almost daily, and if they were not careful, they could become so accustomed to its presence that it could be easy to fail to truly grasp the finality of the impact it had on others, who, because of their vocation, were not accustomed to death visiting daily.

Deaths of loved ones, children, or close acquaintances could leave permanent scars on the most seasoned emergency workers, it was part of being human. For emergency workers to survive many years in a vocation that dealt in life and death almost daily, there needed to be a sense deep inside the individual that would constantly send a message to them personally that what they were doing served a higher good, that at times it made a positive difference in the lives of those they touched. The work removed a living-hell existence from many lives. A spiritual application existed for the presence of this inner awareness that could only be sensed by the recipient. The message travels to the essence of our being, of who we are as spiritual beings.

Jesus spoke these words roughly two thousand years ago:

"If you love me, you will keep my commandments. [16] And I will ask the Father, and he will give you another Helper, to be with you forever, [17] even the Spirit of truth, whom the world cannot receive, because it neither sees him nor knows him. You know him, for he dwells with you and **will be in you** (John 14.15-17).

This Spirit of Truth could become comfort and encouragement to emergency workers. Emergency workers do not need accolades from anyone but their inward being applauding them for a job well done. A life saved might not have happened unless they put on a uniform that day and went to work. Their efforts, combined with an occasional positive outcome, were enough to keep us showing up for work.

CHAPTER 24

Dead Serious

It was early evening, just after supper, an emergency call came in for abdominal pain in one of the downtown hotels. We arrived on scene, grabbed our equipment, and headed into the lobby. A hotel employee took us to the elevators; we went up about twenty floors. Entering the room, we found a middle-aged man and his wife sitting up on the bed. They were tourists from out of town and had just finished eating their evening meal. Sitting up in bed, the man complained of some mild indigestion. We assessed the patient, found nothing unusual, and explained to him that we would be glad to take him to a local hospital in the downtown area to get him checked further. He didn't want to go, he said he'd be fine, but his wife suggested that he should go, and she would meet us at the hospital shortly. We put him in a sitting position on the stretcher and wheeled him down in the elevator and loaded him in the back of the ambulance for transport. It was a beautiful evening. We sat in the back of the ambulance with the doors open, taking in the fresh air. His condition was unchanged since our first contact.

My partner placed the heart leads from the heart monitor on the patient in preparation to transport him to the hospital. I was sitting on the bench seat in the back of the ambulance across from the patient. I began asking him about his medical history and other information as I filled out the patient form for the hospital. I asked him an additional question and he didn't respond right away like he did on all the other questions. I looked up from my form to ask him again when my partner started slamming his fist on top of the heart monitor and cursing because the digital readout was not showing anything close to a normal reading for a conscious patient.

We simultaneously looked from the heart monitor screen back to the patient and noticed our patient was clinically dead. No pulse, no respirations. He died silently during my patient-history questionnaire. No indication of pain, no verbal exchange, no movement on the stretcher, just dead. We immediately began CPR with advanced life support. Upon arrival at the hospital, we transferred the patient to the receiving docs, gave our report to the staff, and watched the hospital continue resuscitation efforts with no change. Eventually they ceased resuscitation efforts and recorded the time of death. His wife was probably still trying to find out what room they put him in, unaware that her life as a widow had just begun.

Not long after this emergency call, we received another. This time it was in our neighborhood not far from the firehouse. The call was for a sick person. We arrived on scene at a small, neat house in a terribly rundown neighborhood. The house looked out of place with the tidiness of the home's curb appeal. We took our equipment to the front door just as an elderly woman, neatly dressed, emerged from the doorway and stepped out onto the porch. She told us she just didn't feel well as she walked toward the ambulance parked on the street in front of her sidewalk. We supported her underneath her arms, helping her walk and she climbed in the ambulance and laid on the stretcher. We began assessing her and prepared her for transport to the hospital. I put a tourniquet on her arm and explained to her that I was going to start an IV on her, that she would feel a little stick, and then I'd be done. I was kneeling on the right side of the stretcher on which she was lying. As I prepared to insert the IV needle I saw her right-hand fold into a fist and her arm muscles tightened. Sensing that she was getting ready to knock me out of my shoes, I moved my free arm across her body so that when she swung her fist, she would just hit my arm. I reassured her that the needle would not hurt that bad and it would be over quickly. She didn't say anything. I watched her fist unfold and her arm relax. I thought she was listening to what I was saying until I looked closer at her face. Her pupils had dilated, and she was no longer breathing. I checked for a pulse, and she had none. She was clinically dead in the five seconds that had elapsed since her fist relaxed.

Again, just like the man with indigestion that died while talking to me, this lady who walked to the ambulance a minute earlier was now dead without making a sound or speaking a word. Like before, we continued with advanced life support all the way to the hospital. She was unresponsive. We passed her to the medical team on standby at the hospital when we arrived; they did everything they could, then stopped resuscitation efforts. The time of death was marked and recorded, and we went back outside, ready for another call.

Later, not the same shift, we got a call to the same park on the edge of downtown where the little boy had drowned months earlier. Two men were parked in a shady area of the park, sharing war stories and drinking. The call was for a sick person. The men were middle aged, sitting outside at a picnic table, drinking. We approached the men and asked who was sick, to which the spokesman said that it was his friend. The friend's remarks were much like the lady that doubled up her fist and died, stating he just didn't feel that great. Honestly, he didn't look that great either. He was pale with clammy skin that glistened with sweat. He was not agitated but acted as though he would rather be left alone. We offered to treat him, but he refused. His friend said he would put him in the back of his car and drive him to get checked out at the hospital. We reluctantly agreed, he signed a refusal-of-treatment form, and we helped him into the car. We went back to our ambulance and began writing up the report while remaining parked on the scene.

I looked out the front windshield of the ambulance at the patient in the back of his friend's car. I told my partner, who was not one of my regular partners, not to drive off yet. This guy didn't look right to me. I got out of the ambulance and walked about thirty feet to the man in the back seat. Sure enough, he was dead. He had died in the back seat as his friend sat in the driver's seat. We pulled his limp body out of the back seat, put him on the stretcher and began life support. It was the same old song, just a different verse. He didn't improve en route or at the hospital. The hospital staff ceased resuscitation efforts and marked the time of death. We got the ambulance ready for the next call.

What do all three of these emergency calls have in common? Several things. None of the patients thought they were going to die that day. All the deaths were sudden, without warning. Resuscitation efforts failed. All seemed pain free, or with such minimal pain that the patient was dead before feeling anything remotely painful. None uttered a word of discomfort when dying. Typically, the heart goes into a type of arrhythmia, or unusual beating pattern, then stops beating. The patient loses consciousness and vital signs disappear. The patient may feel sick, like the man in the park and the lady we met at the front door to her house. The man in the downtown hotel only complained of a feeling of minor indigestion. All had one major thing in common. They were all alive, then without notice, they were gone. No suffering, no time to get things in order, no time to do the things they might have always wanted to do. Bucket lists unfinished. No time to say goodbye. No more time for anything. Game over.

Experts in the field of finance typically say that once a person becomes what would be considered elderly, things like money take on a much lesser role in their lives. The importance of money and getting ahead financially is supplanted by a desire for time. Having more money can work as a goal for the young, but as we age, we realize that time is finite, that the end game is approaching, and time is what matters now. Money cannot buy more time. Wouldn't it be nice to give time its rightful place in the hierarchy of life at an early age, instead of waiting until it's almost gone to give it the respect it deserves? Death, which can happen when we least expect it, has made me understand that whatever we are trying to accomplish in life needs to take a backseat to acknowledging the importance of time, and how it should be valued above almost every other thing we put too much value on. Ask an eighty-five-year-old man or woman how much they value time. The more it gets in short supply, the more it is valued.

Trying to put my thoughts together after the man in the park died, I can't help thinking about the apparition. Thinking about it helps tremendously in trying to make sense of sudden death. It's really not "game over" for any of these patients. The game will continue, just on a different playing field. The apparition would not have appeared to me at all unless there was more to this life than just our physical manifestation on Earth. Most people think of death as entering the unknown. Being unknown, however, doesn't nullify its existence. It's real–waiting to be experienced when we die.

CHAPTER 25

Traditional Tradition

I continued to teach the couples' Bible class at the church every other Sunday. During this time the deacon body removed the current pastor and brought in an interim pastor to preach. Sometimes churches remove pastors the people may not be happy with for whatever reason and tell the congregation that God led the pastor to a different church or occupation, which may or may not be true. The congregation may not be happy with the color of the carpet that the pastor chose, or other similarly serious infractions, so the people go to their deacons, who then have a deacons' meeting and vote to remove the pastor. Because the system of government in a traditional church is so flawed, the pastor-selection process is equally flawed. Typically, the interim pastor who fills in is the one who gets selected to be the new pastor. The interim pastor position is not always filled by a Pulpit Committee, but sometimes selected by a Deacon Board. In this case, that was exactly what happened. The Deacon Board put the interim pastor in place for several months during which time he was on his best behavior preaching non-controversial messages; then a vote was taken. This process is similar to a prisoner trying to get an early release for good behavior, except in reverse.

During the interim pastor's tenure, a faux Pulpit Committee, which may as well be a group of cardboard cutout images depicting committee members sitting around a large table, was drawn up as a search committee to attempt to fill the empty pulpit with a full-time pastor. The pseudo search committee was a lame–duck formality; the Deacon Board put the interim pastor that they had selected to a vote before the congregation and rammed the vote through. By this time, I am really starting to sour on the traditional, denominational, religious experience.

The newly hired pastor was a businessman holding a pastor position. He was intelligent, with the façade of a politician. Very ambitious, it seemed he was trying to build a brick-and-mortar utopia on Earth. It took him a few years, but with stoic determination and a no-quit attitude, he was finally successful in bankrupting the church. Naturally, with the impeccable timing of a looming church bankruptcy, God called him to a different church, this time back to his home state.

The next interim pastor threw a curveball to the Deacon Board. He agreed to preach but would not accept the pastor position. This meant the Pastor Search Committee could search for a spirit-filled pastor without the interim pastor getting the nod. The cardboard cutouts depicting committee members were stored away and a real Pastor Search Committee was able to bring in a wonderful Spirit-filled pastor. He was the opposite of his predecessor. He accepted the pastorship and never asked anyone what his compensation package looked like. He cared nothing about expanding the physical building. He ranked in the lower-middle class and cared nothing for money. He had also experienced spiritual events outside of the boundaries of the traditional, denominational church, which separated him from the business-type pastors.

It took a full two years for the deacon body to run him off–close to a record. The infraction stemmed from his refusal to fire the music minister. The congregation was complaining because they felt the music was too loud, so to get the music minister to feel the calling of God to another church, it was necessary to fire the pastor, too. A two-for-one package deal. Again the deacons, by allowing all their family members to vote, were able to ram the vote through. Deacons' young children who were members of the church, with the promise of a red snow cone later, voted as the parents said to vote and the process was done.

When they fired the pastor, I went with him, and we started a new church with several other people who left as well. I had finally reached my saturation point with traditional, denominational religion.

This time around, the fired pastor started a non-denominational, non-traditional church. Twenty years later it was still thriving with the same pastor. The church had no Deacon Board and no business meetings. The church congregation did not have a vote on anything. Basically, if you were not happy with the church he was now pastoring, you had the option to go find another church down the road.

Had I not witnessed the apparition and been shown another world, I may have been totally satisfied with the traditional religious experience. This didn't happen. I knew there was more. Seeing the apparition had given me a passion for seeking, and consequently discovering, more. Discovering that a church body contains a smorgasbord of different types of people in different stages of spirituality. Discovering that all the people were in different stages of spiritual growth, having different spiritual goals, or no goals at all. Discovering that some had visions for a church body or community, or no vision at all. Discovering that we were all flawed and desperately needed God. Discovering that I was not content to go through the motions of a religious experience anymore. Instead, I sought relationship.

CHAPTER 26

Let Me Guess, "Two Beers"

A sk any drunk driver how much they have had to drink, and the standard answer is always, "Two beers." They may have just totaled their car or injured others, fatally or otherwise, and it's always the same answer. It doesn't matter if they can't even stand up, much less walk. This answer took me back to my basic on-the-job training as a new paramedic. We were taught the number-one rule when working the streets as a paramedic is: The patient always lies. Rule number two: See rule number one.

The emergency calls for alcohol-related emergencies started coming back-to-back with no breaks. We got the next call for a single-vehicle traffic accident close to our district. The bars were starting to close now, so the drunks were driving around trying to find more alcohol instead of going home. Arriving at the vehicle accident we saw a late- model Camaro had struck a utility pole with such force that the pole was sheared off with the car coming to rest on top of what was left of the utility pole—a two-foot-tall wooden stump sticking out of the sidewalk.

Taking care to avoid the electrically charged wires that were dancing in the street, I tried gaining access to the driver, who was slumped over the steering wheel and not moving. The driver's door was crumpled to the point of not being able to open it, so I went to the passenger door, it opened easily, and I climbed in the front passenger seat to assess the driver. She appeared to be about twenty years old and not moving. No one else was in the car. I could see that she was still breathing. Her face was slumped over the steering wheel, hidden by long thick, black, curly hair flowing down her back and face. I put a BP cuff on her arm and began inflating it. Before I could immobilize her and get an accurate blood pressure, she began slowly raising her head. She turned slowly toward me. Blood oozed from her mouth and flowed down her chin. Her teeth appeared loose, folded toward the back of her mouth. Her large, brown, glassy, bloodshot eyes were trying to focus on me without success. In a low, raspy voice, still trying to focus her eyes on me, she moved her mouth awkwardly, as if she was coming off anesthesia in the dentist's office. The words came slowly. Finally, she spoke. The message was clear and concise. She asked me if I wanted to drive.

When the weather was nice in the evening, the firefighters and paramedics would sit in front of the firehouse in wooden, Adirondack chairs waiting for the next emergency call. This evening, neighborhood prostitutes came by the firehouse to chat. There were three or four of them, one just arriving from New York. New to the neighborhood, the New Yorker was trying to get the firefighters to take her up on her offer to get on the stretcher in the back of the ambulance parked in the bay. She wanted forty dollars. I don't know what goes on in New York City but there are no firefighters I know willing to lose their jobs so she can make forty dollars. The ladies moved on down the street just as an emergency call for a laceration came in.

We arrived on scene and there were what appeared to be two young women, one bleeding from the face. They were both dressed nicely, and accessorized in jewelry, purses and high heels. They were overdressed for the neighborhood. I put the one with the facial laceration in the captain's chair facing the rear of the ambulance, the other on the bench seat. The facial lacerations came from someone using a broken beer bottle as a weapon to the face. While I bandaged her face, a female police officer opened the back doors of the ambulance so she could gather information about the assault. The police officer recognized the patient right away and called her Juan. I said, "Juan, not Juanita?" The police officer told him and his friend to get out of our ambulance and quit wasting the paramedic's time. I finished bandaging his face, then both men picked up their purses and exited the ambulance. I was shocked that they were men. I had inadvertently mistaken these men for women. Sometimes it's easier for me to tell if they're men by the lower tone of voice, larger adams apple on the neck, and manly looking hands, but honestly, these guys looked beautiful. Beautiful, yes, women, no. I could see how any intoxicated man would think he had won the lottery escorting them to his motel room. The real surprise would come later, and that sometimes resulted in another emergency call for an assault. As soon as our patients exited the ambulance, a call came in for an assault at a bar.

We arrived on scene and went into the bar looking for the patient. The bar was full of people participating in deferring their problems with excessive alcohol consumption. The patrons postponed their problems, at least until tomorrow, when the problems returned accompanied by a roaring hangover. The music and crowd were loud. Patrons yelled at each other as they tried to carry on a conversation over the music, using worn-out pick-up lines through slurred speech. An employee pointed us to the rear of the bar that led out through a back exit. We went outside behind the bar; the assaulted victim was lying on his back, alone on a picnic table, barely conscious, moaning, with multiple stab wounds in his torso. He was a big man–sweaty, tough looking, with a huge barrel chest covered by a bloody, long-sleeved shirt with the sleeves rolled part way up his arms. His long sleeves would only roll up two flips of the cuff before the thickness of his forearms made it impossible to roll higher. The top three buttons on his shirt were unbuttoned, revealing a gold neck chain with a medallion of the Virgin Mary of Guadalupe. The manner in which he wore his shirt, with the sleeves up and the chest area uncovered, revealed a possible reason why he was now laying on the picnic table, barely alive. Exposing his muscular physique by bearing his arms and chest could have been an attempt to send an enticing, subliminal message to women in the dancehall that he was a fine specimen to mate with, potentially producing strong healthy offspring. His exposed gold chain could send another message to females: I've got a job; I'm not poor, and I would be able to take care of you. I'm also religious, as evidenced by the Virgin Mary medallion. I'm quite the catch.

Thick black hair with too much oil–he must have had a father like mine–covered his head. A large handlebar mustache that somehow connected with his sideburns, rounded out the look of his still, motionless face.

His attempt to attract the opposite sex seemed to have backfired on him. I had seen it happen a few other times while working the streets. His ego, derived from his big, virile, muscular appearance and the effort he put in to accessorizing his mate-attraction garb, gave him the confidence to cast his gaze on a female target one millisecond too long. Other male patrons may have noted his interest in a woman that they were also interested in. The mating ritual as old as time had begun. The game, designed to eliminate the competition, had no rules. If the intruder was large and strong, a group would take him out of the contest instead of an individual trying it alone. It was rarely a fair fight, the objective was just to remove him from the suitable-mate list in any way possible.

Lying on his back, alone, behind the dancehall, unable to talk, bleeding out from his multiple stab wounds, I suspected that the mating ritual was over for the big man. I was thinking it had taken more than one man to put this big moose on his back. He had lost a lot of blood. Obviously, someone had called 911, but being dumped on a picnic table behind the bar with multiple stab wounds was an indicator that nobody really cared if he lived or died, as the loud music and partying seemed to take precedence over his present predicament. We loaded him up in the ambulance, tended to emergency-care duties, and took him to the hospital. We delivered him alive to the trauma department, gave our report to the docs and nurses, then got back in service.

Immediately the next call came in as another assault. We arrived at a bar where several in the neighborhood liked to dance and party. The music was Tejano with Spanish lyrics. The large dance floor was crowded with patrons, twirling and whirling. Nothing changed as we entered the front door of the bar. Everyone was still dancing, as if they were all in a musical trance. No one looked our way. No one appeared to care who we were or why we were there. It was as close to invisible as I've ever felt. We walked across the dance floor, lugging our medical equipment and bumping into entranced dancers.

The patient was lying in a pool of blood in the middle of the dance floor. He seemed alone in a sea of uncaring humanity. The dancers would only look toward him when they danced too close, trying to avoid stepping in his blood, or tripping over him. They whirled and twirled, oblivious to everything but the location of the blood that pooled around him. He appeared to have been beaten badly, not moving, unconscious, but still alive. No one was attending to his injuries, he was as invisible as we were, as if we were all a mirage. We managed to load him in the ambulance. No one asked if he was okay, or what hospital we were going to. It was as if he only existed as a nuisance, an irritation to patrons who wanted to forget their lives.

Getting drunk while whirling and twirling until the sun came up, they would drive away erratically, unsteadily, with a mental deception that they were the best drivers on the planet. Seeing double of everything, running over curbs, trashcans, and everything else near the roadway with no recollection. They stumbled into their shacks, sweaty drunk, stinking of stale alcohol and cheap cologne, with salt stains on their shirts from sweating while dancing all night, and broke. Many left the bar with someone they met at the dancehall only to wake up hungover and head pounding, next to a stranger whose name they couldn't remember. Time to shower and go to work to earn enough money to do it again next weekend. The nihilistic attitudes of some were on full display in the neighborhood dancehalls in our district.

Leaving the hospital, another call came in for an injured party with no specific information. I loathed these types of calls because the call could be for anything, there was no way to mentally prepare for what we might encounter. The location was another bar, but this bar was a neighborhood bar with lots of revelers getting intoxicated, but like an independent Baptist church, no dancing allowed. This bar had a reputation for serving good food. They served one of the best chicken fried steaks in the city. One of the wait staff led us into the kitchen. In the corner of the kitchen area was a young man, a waiter, clutching his hand in a paper towel as blood ran down his arm. I removed the paper towel to discover his index finger had been severed. The severed end of the finger was also missing. I asked him where the end of his finger was, so we could possibly get it reattached at the hospital. The patient explained that he was using his index finger to force the ice to flow better in the margarita machine when his finger was severed. The end of the finger was still in the margarita machine. I looked toward the machine where other servers were still filling margarita glasses.

Evidently, no one knew or cared whether there was a finger in the margarita machine. We bandaged his hand and unplugged the margarita machine. We told the bar owner not to serve anymore margaritas, and the young man said he would ride to the hospital with his friend. I mentally scratched this place off my list as a future dining destination. We finished the run, got back in service, and started heading back to the firehouse. I already suspected the bar owner had probably plugged the margarita machine back in without permission. Can't miss out on sales on a busy night like tonight. Once we left, it was likely business as usual for the bar. Keep the alcohol flowing. Keep the patrons happy. Make a profit. The apathy of humanity began to overwhelm me. If we, myself and the rest of humanity, were all in this together, why the uncaring attitude of some of the masses?

The stabbing victim was left alone to die on a picnic table behind the bar.

The unconscious, bloody man, left to die in the middle of a dance floor with uncaring people dancing all around him.

The wait staff at the last bar still served margaritas with the severed finger in the margarita machine. Granted, some of the wait staff may not have known the finger was in the machine, but the nine-fingered man knew. He could have said something. Some people only cared about themselves and made it very hard for the ones who did care for others. Uncaring people were seemingly fine with their apathetic attitudes as long as their own lives were working out for them.

It has been my experience that real friends, true friends, were those that were truly happy for you when successes came. They helped in suffering and felt your pain; they sincerely wanted things to improve for you. I feel fortunate to have had a few real friends in the past, they are so rare. Typically, real friends can be counted on one hand.

I wondered if it was the misery, hardship, and suffering in life that made some people become bitter and uncaring. If that were true, then wouldn't all the people in dire straits become bitter, callous, and uncaring? Yet, they don't. Some thrived in suffering. Some starving prisoners in World War II prison camps shared their less-than-meager rations with fellow prisoners. *Why? Why did some men give up their seats in the lifeboats on the sinking Titanic so that women and children would be saved, when other men did not? Why did some firefighters who had already made one trip inside the collapsing Twin Towers in New York City go back in to try to rescue more people, most realizing it was suicide to do so?* The only answer was that they cared. They cared about people they never met. Other peoples' lives were worth something; they had value. Those who knew this, valued others because they knew there was more to this life than meets the eye. Knowing there was a spiritual world out there provided hope, and this hope could carry us through the worst of suffering, even death. The apparition equipped me with this hope.

CHAPTER 27

Really?

Two things rookie paramedics learn on the streets, or should learn, is to always show respect to their patients. In poor neighborhoods, especially in neighborhoods where most people were struggling for survival, respect was not only given, but demanded. To disrespect someone, especially in front of family members and friends, was to rain hell down on your own head. Be ready for a fight. It's ok to laugh at a situation or something the patient says, as in the lady asking me if I wanted to drive, but never laugh at them during the patient-paramedic interaction. The paramedic must always remain professional, even if the interaction was hilarious.

A thirty-year-old lady walked into the fire station for help. It was morning and we were sitting around the kitchen table drinking coffee after a long night. She was in terrible distress, crying and digging in her ear. A roach had taken up residence in her ear canal. Each time it moved, she screamed. We tilted her head so that the roach would be closest to the floor and began irrigating the ear with saline and a squeeze bulb. After several unsuccessful attempts at irrigation the lady stopped our efforts. She said, "Why don't you try flushing it out by irrigating the opposite ear?" Well trained firefighter-paramedics continued irrigation without laughing or demeaning her.

The time to laugh was when the patient had already been dropped off at the hospital. Paramedics and firefighters develop a warped sense of humor. The firehouse banter between fire paramedics and firefighters inside the firehouse can make a very serious accident scene or fire into a hilarious discussion. One especially beneficial coping mechanism used by first responders to stave off post-traumatic stress was to turn tragedy into comedy. I know it may sound sick, but it really helped in carrying the emotional load of overwhelming tragedy. To an outsider, it may seem callous and uncaring. For me, I have found it takes the edge off.

CHAPTER 28

The Truth Will Set You Free

The new church, with the pastor that had been fired from our old church, began to flourish spiritually. It never did grow to be a large church, but the congregants grew in the Word and in the Spirit. I stayed on as an adult Bible teacher, with the same co-teacher that I had rotated with bi-weekly at the old church. We were close friends, the kind of friends where we could sit in silence and understand each other without words. These types of friends were extremely rare.

There were spiritual battles all the time. I learned that if a church is truly being what God would have it to be, the enemy, Satan, would always come against it. The attacks were relentless at times, but God allowed us to weather every storm. People would come from anywhere and everywhere, bringing their own belief system with them. This was fine, it showed me that they were seeking truth. God's Holy Spirit draws people to truth. One characteristic of the Holy Spirit, there are many, is Teacher. He guides us into truth. I needed this guidance to truth as much as those who were new truth seekers in our congregation. Lining up with the truth of God's Word is a never-ending process of transformation that occurs gradually over time. We are all in different stages of transformation.

I learned never to be judgmental of another person because they might not have reached the level of transformation as someone else. None of us have it all figured out. A church, every church, is a congregation of sinners. If there were such a thing as a perfect church there would be no way people would be allowed in. We are all flawed sinners. We become Christians only through God's grace; we do nothing to earn our salvation. The Holy Spirit draws us, Jesus saves us, and God receives us as one of His children. We do nothing except receive our new position as one of God's children through faith because of the sacrifice Jesus made on the cross when He died to pay the price for my sin and yours.

Humans have a propensity for evil and unprecedented, malevolent behavior. Who could say Hitler or Stalin were good people? It's part of our nature as human beings. We were born this way. Ask a two-year-old if he ate a chocolate candy bar and he will lie to your face with his hands and face smeared with chocolate. Christians, as much as anyone else, have this propensity to sin, to commit evil acts against each other. It is our nature.

The Apostle Paul explains it in the scriptures.

[15] For I do not understand my own actions. For I do not do what I want, but I do the very thing I hate. [16] Now if I do what I do not want, I agree with the law, that it is good. [17] So now it is no longer I who do it, but sin that dwells within me. [18] For I know that nothing good dwells in me, that is, in my flesh. For I have the desire to do what is right, but not the ability to carry it out. [19] For I do not do the good I want, but the evil I do not want is what I keep on doing. [20] Now if I do what I do not want, it is no longer I who do it, but sin that dwells within me.

²¹ So I find it to be a law that when I want to do right, evil lies close at hand. ²² For I delight in the law of God, in my inner being, ²³ but I see in my members another law waging war against the law of my mind and making me captive to the law of sin that dwells in my members. ²⁴ Wretched man that I am! Who will deliver me from this body of death? (Rom. 17.15-24).

As believers, will we still sin and commit evil? Unfortunately, yes, even when we don't want to. But the debt for our sin has already been paid. The truth that evil exists in all of us is a stumbling block for people who think they are basically good human beings. They will keep trying hard to make sure they are good, even while knowing they are not. Pride interferes with acknowledging that a Savior has come, but the Scriptures are clear on the matter. God has a plan to redeem humankind. Let Him. When God rewrites our story, it has a redemptive ending.

CHAPTER 29

Just When You Think You've Seen Everything

Veteran paramedics will say that once you have worked in a working firehouse as a paramedic for six months, you will have seen just about every type of emergency possible. I don't necessarily agree with that, after six months, there were still plenty more to come.

A man drove his pickup truck to our firehouse, got out and walked in to seek assistance. He was weather-beaten, hungover, looking to be in his late forties or early fifties. He was in distress, complaining that his stomach hurt. After assessing him and taking a history, it turned out that he had been with a neighborhood prostitute. He had passed out and woke up later, alone and with abdominal pain, so he drove himself to the firehouse for help. While doing a patient assessment on him, auscultating and palpating his abdomen, a vibration would occur about every ten seconds lasting two to three seconds. It was easy to feel the vibration with a hand on the stomach area. The vibration emanated primarily from the lower abdomen, so there was a good chance of a battery powered device in there somewhere.

Before taking him to the hospital, we used this patient as a training tool for a new rookie firefighter to gain some experience in patient assessment. I asked the rookie to recheck the patient without telling the rookie what we had already discovered. I'll never forget the look on the rookie's face when the vibration occurred while he was listening to the patient's abdominal area with a stethoscope. Priceless.

Before the patient had a chance to return to the firehouse to retrieve his pickup truck, a car sped into the back parking lot of the firehouse where the patient's truck was parked. Coming to a screeching stop, a woman jumped out of the car and began throwing clothes all over the parking lot around the pickup. She then jumped into her car and sped away.

The patient returned later to retrieve his pickup truck. He showed us x-rays of a large cucumber shaped device that had been inserted in his rectum. It must have had fresh batteries in it, causing it to continually vibrate periodically for hours. He said the doctors had a difficult time removing it, but eventually they were successful. We told him that a lady had delivered his clothes while he was at the hospital. He nodded his head and left.

CHAPTER 30

Diabetic Emergencies

When working in a city of over a million people, there's a good chance of responding to calls for people suffering from low blood sugar, insulin shock in some cases. Most of these calls originate from callers who say something is wrong with their friend or family member, they just aren't acting right.

The first one such call came from someone who became suspicious of a man riding the elevator in a high-rise building. We arrived at the building address, primarily used by petroleum company executives, and proceeded up the elevator to the designated floor. A lady led us to the patient, who was riding the elevator. When the elevator door opened, a sharply dressed executive man wearing a business suit was standing alone in the elevator with a leather briefcase on the floor next to him. We entered the elevator with him. He pushed the button for another floor without anyone saying a word, then we all rode in silence to the floor he had selected. The door opened and he did not get off, but pushed a button to select another floor. We rode in silence to the designated floor, the door opened and again he silently, stoically, stood without moving. We told him this was his floor, and ushered him out of the elevator, taking a seat in the lobby.

I went to the closest vending machine and found him a candy bar. Convincing him to eat, we all sat there, in silence, for about ten minutes and watched him chew each bite about a hundred times before swallowing. Eventually, the petroleum executive's brain began functioning, he became alert and oriented. He looked at his watch and ascertained that he had been riding the elevator up and down for over an hour, oblivious to everything and everyone. It amazes me how dangerously low blood sugar can cause the brain to take an unscheduled vacation.

On another emergency call, we arrived on the edge of the city where the call originated. We looked around trying to find the emergency. Finally, we spotted a plowed field, where one would normally see a farmer's tractor pulling a plow or other type of farming implement. In this case, it was a man in a nice dress shirt and tie driving the family sedan through the plowed field. He was driving perpendicular to the plowed furrows, his car bumping up and down like a carnival ride, as he traveled about three mph over each furrow through the field. The driver's window was down, so we briskly walked next to his car and asked him what he was doing. He didn't look at us or respond, but kept his eyes focused straight ahead with both hands on the steering wheel to avoid any accidents while driving in the field. My partner reached through the open window and turned the key off, stopping the car. The driver never looked at us or said anything. He kept his hands on the wheel, facing forward, body erect as if he was taking a driving test. Yep, low blood sugar again. As soon as the sugar level was restored, he was a cognitive adult with a car in serious need of a wheel alignment. He was now missing an hour of memory he would never get back.

One of my most memorable diabetic emergencies came on a warm, humid afternoon with no breeze. We got the call for an "unknown" in the neighborhood close to the firehouse, which was usually bad because there was no time to mentally prepare for what we might find while responding to the scene. We arrived in a grocery-store parking lot, with people moving their cars and shopping carts all over the parking lot while this large, middle-aged woman was lying on her back in the middle of the lot.

Her contagious laugh seemed uncontrollable. No one was paying any attention to her, which I thought was odd because she was loud. I walked over to her and squatted down next to her with my shadow shielding her face from the bright sun. Her skin was black, her clothes were black, and the parking lot surface was black. I knew she must have been hot lying in the sun. Her wig, looking like a small, black, furry animal, was lying on the black asphalt about four feet away. She was laughing so hard that tears were running down her face. Her laugh was loud and deep, a continuous Santa Claus laugh with an Aretha Franklin tone that changed pitch as if melodic.

I leaned my head down really close to her face and asked her if she hurt or felt any pain. She looked me straight in the eyes, stopped laughing, then at the top of her lungs she shouted, "I feels [sic] good like a big dog!" We took her to the hospital, still laughing her head off, as we administered IV D50, (dextrose in a water-soluble solution), en route.

Probably the worst case of sugar levels dropping to a dangerous level came from a lady who lived in our response district. A friend, unable to contact her, called 911 because she was worried that something was wrong. We arrived at the house, no one came to the door, so we went in and found her in the bathtub. She was lying naked in the bathtub, unconscious, with snoring respirations. We could not wake her or move her. She was a large woman, over three hundred pounds; her body filled every part of the empty tub. Somehow the water had drained out of the tub. After acquiring extra man-power from a fire crew, we were able to free her from the tub without injury. Wrapping her in a blanket, we put her on the stretcher in the ambulance and started an IV line. Normally one vial of D50 is enough to wake the patient. This patient required several vials.

Once she was awake and alert in the back of the ambulance, I asked her what happened. She said she had filled the tub with water this evening and started taking a bath. She started feeling weak and must have passed out. I asked her what time she started her bath because it was late afternoon on Sunday and she had said she bathed in the evening. She replied that she started bathing on Friday evening. She was shocked when I told her it was Sunday afternoon. She had been in the bathtub for almost two days.

I mention these low-blood-sugar emergencies because paramedics treat them quite often, typically every shift. It's a very common emergency. The fascinating thing about these types of emergencies is that once the brain's sugar level gets too low, it doesn't function well. Reality becomes skewed; in extreme cases the patient loses consciousness. All cognitive functions become dramatically altered. Rational thinking grinds to a halt.

I began to think about how life could be so fragile. Low blood sugar dramatically alters cognitive function to the point of unconsciousness, rendering a patient totally helpless. Sometimes there is no response to painful stimuli, no awareness or orientation to time or space, like waking from surgery and having no knowledge of what happened for the hours spent on the operating table. When experiencing a low-blood-sugar emergency the patient can lose consciousness. This unconscious patient enters a state of pain-free existence, not yet dead, but not awake. This state of unconsciousness is a respite from the pain, misery, and suffering of life, yet we fear any transition to death where we are no longer in control. I've concluded that it isn't the transfer process from life to death that terrifies most people, it's the anxiety associated with traversing into the unknown. We all prefer having a semblance of control over our own life, yet this process allows for no control. Since viewing the apparition, the fear of death doesn't really bother me anymore. It has given me great comfort, especially seeing repeatedly how life is so transient.

CHAPTER 31

The Transience of Life

"How do you know what your life will be like tomorrow? Your life is like the morning fog—it's here a little while, then it's gone" (James 4.14).

The midday emergency call still haunts my sleep at night. There is a park close to the downtown area that has a river running through it. It is a beautiful area, lush, green, quiet, and peaceful. There are paddle boats that tourists can rent and enjoy paddling the boats around the river.

The call came in for a possible drowning. We arrived on the scene to find a hysterical mother standing on the bank crying, yelling, and screaming in anguish. The usually quiet, peaceful park was far from peaceful today. Mom had been pedaling a paddle boat in the river when her four-year-old little boy had slipped off the paddle boat into the river. He never surfaced; he was still underwater, somewhere. The water was murky, with a mild current. Cypress trees lined the banks, with large roots extending into the river. Cat tails and lily pads further complicated visibility under the water.

Mom frantically pointed out the location of the tragedy when the rescue dive team arrived and quickly began search and rescue. We waited. It was taking too long to find him. The water was fresh water instead of salt water, which helped his survivability, but the water temperature was not cold enough to sufficiently slow his metabolism, which exacerbated his need for oxygen.

Time was everything. Mom was going to pieces. Trying to comfort and reassure Mom as time ticked away seemed more and more like false assurances.

"The divers are well trained, and they are doing everything they can," we offered. "Hopefully they will find him soon."

Ten minutes went by, twenty, thirty, I felt heavy dread while I tried to keep a stoic, positive demeanor for Mom, who had stopped screaming and was crying quietly. My outside demeanor revealed nothing but trained composure, a learned behavior from experiencing too many overwhelming tragedies in my job. With each additional minute the boy was underwater, I began dying on the inside.

Mom's quiet crying and anguish was wearing on my attempt to remain emotionally unattached. Cognitive compartmentalization, which I had mastered, could only hold the dam of emotion back so long, it too, had a breaking point. I filed the pain and dread in one compartment so I could perform my job, while drawing from another compartment labeled training. I was hurting so badly for her. The longer he stayed under water, the slimmer his chances of survival.

Finally, a diver surfaced with the boy and threw him into my arms. He wore a shirt and little blue jeans held up by a belt with an oversized cowboy belt buckle. He had little boots on his feet. The boots were the type of boots I had recently bought for my four-year-old son. The toes of his boots were worn, the leather all scuffed, just like the toes of my son's boots. My son would use the toes of his boots to drag on the concrete to slow his bicycle. This boy's lips were blue, his face ashen gray. He could easily have passed for my son if he weren't so hypoxic. I put him in the back of the ambulance.

My partner and I immediately began advanced life support en route to the hospital. He was not responding to treatment.

My raw emotion was being suppressed, to be dealt with later, if ever, so I could work, but it was slowly manifesting itself as anger. I was starting to get so angry at the situation and was struggling with *why?* We arrived at the hospital, gave the report to the doctors, and the medical team took over life-support efforts. Nothing had changed, the boy was still clinically dead. I walked out of the trauma room and the boy's mom and dad met me wanting a report of how their son was doing. Trained to respond in these situations, I told them the doctors were doing everything they could do. I already suspected he was dead, but the doctors were literally giving the little boy every chance at recovery that they possibly could. The doctors stopped resuscitation efforts. The boy had passed.

I got in the back of the ambulance. I started throwing away all the used, disposable, life-support equipment and cleaning up the stretcher. I put another clean disposable sheet on the stretcher and threw away the wet stretcher sheet that smelled like the river. Black, clay, riverbank mud covered the floor in the back of the ambulance from mine and my partner's boots. I scrubbed on the mud, already operating on autopilot, numb, unfeeling, and robotic. I started writing my report. It was time to get back in service for another emergency call. Too much time at the hospital and the dispatcher came over the radio wanting us to get back in service for another run. My adrenalin was spent. All I could think about was the little boy's boots being exactly like the ones I bought for my own son. I struggled with the gnawing question: *Why is my son alive, and this little boy is dead? Why? Did his parents deserve to lose their son?* No, no one deserves that. *Did I deserve to have a living son?* Parents had nothing to do with this tragedy. He was a healthy little boy who never even had a chance at life. His life was over before he even had a chance to live it.

When this little boy drowned, I had been working as a paramedic in the fire department for several years. I had witnessed so many people die, of every age, but children's deaths were always the ones that left scars for life. Veteran paramedics would tell me that the scars never leave. It's true, you learn and grow, but never forget. The details stay with you always. I have personally found this to be true. For years after this incident, I made my children wear life jackets when near the water. I was the life jacket nazi until they swam like professionals. My kids could have taken the gold in swimming in the Olympics, but the life jackets would probably have slowed them down.

Death does not discriminate. From crib to elderly, death seems to be so random. Indiscriminate death, no security or insulation from the prospect of ceasing to exist on this planet tomorrow, today, or this very minute. There is no guarantee any of us will continue in this life. Death will take us all at various ages and in a variety of ways. Atheists believe in nothingness after death. Many religious people aren't sure of anything after death, but have hope that their theory is correct, whatever it is. With over two hundred religions in the world, this decreases the odds that the version of the afterlife to which one aspires is correct. Dwell on the transience of life for more than a minute and it can take you to dark places. Hopelessness can set in, understandably, given the situation in which we all find ourselves. For me, in the occupation I have chosen, my saving grace has been the realization that there is more to this life than the physical realm in which we exist. It's a good thing knowing this, for without this knowledge, it would seem the suicide rate would be astronomical. A spiritual realm exists, which points to a Creator existing outside creation. Witnessing the apparition has shown me clear evidence of this fact, allowing me to exist in this world without a totally nihilistic, malevolent worldview. I still hurt, who wouldn't? Emergency calls like the one where this little boy drowned continue to haunt my subconscious. It's more bearable with time, but even with time, it never leaves. It's like a despised visitor that comes to visit once a week, in the middle of the night, in the middle of deep slumber, that gnaws at the subconscious. *What could have been done differently to create a positive outcome? Would it have helped if I had gone into the water instead of relying on the divers? Is there something, anything, that I missed that I could have done better?*

CHAPTER 32

Hi Honey, I'm Home

Working as a paramedic taught me so many things about the human condition. Suffering, misery, and tragedy were the norm. Malevolent tendencies surfaced, directed even to those we professed to love, if only just to hurt them to steal what they have. Assaulting one's own mother with the motive of stealing money from her purse to buy drugs is a form of sick, desperate survival for addicts on the streets. We are all trapped in this mess together.

Veteran paramedics would tell me that happiness went out of their lives the moment they started working the streets. So much tragedy, it became unbearable at times, causing a form of PTSD that never got treated, except in conversations with other firefighter-paramedics. Healing occurs in these conversations, only because you know that they know; they lived it as well. Talking to a spouse or family member or friend was no help, knowing they couldn't possibly understand. Coming home after twenty emergency calls in twenty-four hours, half being horrendous, and meeting your spouse's question of, "How was your shift?" with a barely audible, "Fine," had no healing.

Perhaps this was the reason so many paramedics, firefighters, and police officers divorced. The percentages for divorce were much higher in these three career fields than the average divorce rate. I would come home from a busy 24-hour shift, beyond tired, wanting nothing more than sleep, which wouldn't come because of all the caffeine consumed trying to make it through the shift. Walking in the front door of the house, my wife wanted to talk about her day, the children wanted to play with daddy, and all daddy wanted to do was sleep. To stave off sleep much longer would drive up the crankiness meter even more. Kindness and compassion had been used up on the job, all that was left was a shell of a man operating on autopilot. Lying in bed, so unbelievably tired. Eyes wide open watching the sun rise even higher in the sky. Finally sleep would come. This kind of sleep was a stupor of drooling blackness, no dreams, short lived, maybe three to four hours. Waking at around noon, still tired, with a fogginess in the brain that caused an inability to know who I was until I looked at my name on my driver's license. Ringing in the ears, no appetite, needing a shower, but not wanting to move. Here come the kids again, daddy's awake. The afternoon seemed to pass with no energy or drive to do anything. Night comes, try to go to bed early. The phone would ring at 5:30 am. It would be the Shift Commander wanting me to come back to work by 7:00 am to work an overtime shift. So much for family time; I have bills to pay.

Some wives of firefighter-paramedics seem unhappy. Their husbands evolve into someone they don't even know anymore. No life outside of emergency medical care, no time for hearing her problems or helping with the kids. Many times, she decides to leave, understandably, wanting a divorce. The wife of my first paramedic partner left him by writing it in lipstick on the bathroom mirror while he was at work. She divorced him and took their son. My other partner never married. When I moved to another ambulance, I gained two new partners. One was trying to stay married, the other was recently divorced and already remarried and having problems in the new relationship. It also ended in divorce. His first wife left him because she said she needed more space, so after the divorce she moved back in with her mother. We all had a good laugh over that one. The second one just left him, after he paid for her college education, and she got his house in the settlement. We all had another good laugh. I told him the next time he wanted to get married to just find a woman he hated and buy her a house. Same outcome without having to mail out wedding invitations.

CHAPTER 33

Even the Golden Hour is Gray

There was no set formula for working in this environment. Learning the fundamentals in paramedic school, with no preparation for working in neighborhoods where I worked in the 1980s, the fundamentals were just that, fundamentals. The city gave paramedics standard-operating procedures to follow when doing the job of a firefighter- paramedic. The standards were written and precise. Black and white, with no deviation from these standards allowed without negative repercussions. The only problem was that there was nothing about the actual job that could be followed to the letter without deviating into gray areas. The city knew this but expected the paramedics to figure out how to make things work without out causing liability to the city. Consequently, we continually operated in a gray area that no paramedic discussed, except with other paramedics.

High-speed-vehicle accidents were an area with a large percentage of gray area. This was because of the life-or-death nature of these types of calls. Head-on collisions were the worst, mainly because of the carnage and death produced by these types of collisions. By doubling the actual impact speed caused by "head ons," it created a whole different type of emergency. These impacts have a higher probability of more casualties, and a low survivability rate, due to the sheer force of instantaneous deceleration. The first thing a paramedic student was taught was to do no harm. "Do no harm" is attributed to the Hippocratic Oath, but it is not really a part of the oath. Whether a part of the oath or not, it was drilled into the head of every new paramedic. The paramedic should be taught instead to save as many lives as possible by whatever means necessary. This would keep paramedics from operating in gray areas almost every shift.

The second thing complicating treating victims of head-ons is what was known as the "golden hour." The "golden hour" is a term often used when describing trauma to suggest that an injured patient has sixty minutes from time of injury to receive definitive care, after which morbidity and mortality significantly increase. This is important as trauma is the leading cause of death under the age of forty years in developed countries. Combining "do no harm" with the truth of the golden hour will almost inevitably cause good paramedics to operate in the gray.

In the 1980s extrication tools were not nearly as sophisticated as they are today. We had the jaws of life and pinch and pry bars, chains and jacks, but when dealing with trapped victims in a high-speed, head-on collision, extrication was sometimes a lengthy process. Therein lies the dilemma. To render aid and extricate a patient from a mangled vehicle, and to get them to a hospital for surgery within the confines of the golden hour, was very difficult at times.

The golden hour begins when the injury occurs. Emergency vehicles get dispatched as soon as the accident is reported but may take a while to arrive on scene due to traffic conditions, distance, and road conditions. By the time accident victims are assessed and triaged, the golden hour has diminished considerably. Triage refers to sorting the patients by priority level, with the highest priorities being handled first. Dead patients receive no priority. Other non-life-threatening injuries such as a broken arm, or what is classified as walking wounded, were given the least priority.

Since extrication can take quite a bit of time off the clock, crash victims were treated in the vehicle while extrication is occurring. Airways, c-spine and bleeding are managed in the vehicle whenever possible, but many of these patients needed immediate surgery and blood replacement to survive. So, what if the patient with a chance of survival is denied that chance due to lengthy extrication? This is part of the job no one talks about, except paramedics amongst themselves.

Sometimes the dashboard area of the wrecked vehicle is so crushed that it pins the patients' legs in the car. The unconscious patient begins losing the battle with the golden hour as their vital signs rapidly diminish. The paramedic has only two choices. Wait until the patient is completely freed from the vehicle, at which time you may be dealing with a corpse, or physically manipulate the lower legs until they can be freed from the wreckage. The latter takes place when a paramedic crawls into the floorboard of the car and physically manipulates lower legs, ankles, and feet until the lower legs are free.

The bystanders only know that the patient is now free to be removed from the vehicle, onlookers do not know what had to take place to make this happen. Taking a live patient to the hospital with a chance of survival, but with injured feet or ankle bones, is more of a justification for decisive action than the alternative of throwing a blanket over a deceased occupant still trapped in the car. All veteran paramedics know this; some have done it many times to save lives. This life-saving action does not fit into a training manual or narrative for the news media at the scene of the accident. The "golden hour" trumps "do no harm."

If I were the person involved in a serious vehicle accident, I would want a paramedic who is willing to operate in the gray area to save my life, even If I walked with a limp after recovery.

As I said earlier, many head-on collisions contain mostly fatalities due to the sheer force of the doubling of the deceleration. In one case, I arrived on scene, being a new paramedic, and discovered the driver was already dead. He was wearing blue jeans and work boots. The blue jeans were torn open lengthwise from just below the hips to below the knees. The work boots were split open at the seam from the top of the boots in the mid-calf area all the way to the foot. I asked my partner about the damaged clothing. He told me that I would occasionally see this. It is caused by the fleshy part of the legs being forced downward toward the feet with such extreme deceleration force that it shreds the blue jeans and rips the boots. Loosely fitting shoes will come off. Talking to students about the danger of alcohol and driving, or other drugs and driving, can never influence them as much as seeing the aftermath of a head-on collision and seeing what the occupants really look like. It's life changing.

CHAPTER 34

Seeing is Believing

After doing my job for years, one thing became embedded in my psyche more than any other: the temporary state of mankind. We may live for a year or ninety years, but we all die. We leave the Earth at death, the physical flesh dies and immediately begins to decay. Our soul continues. All souls continue. My souls' continuance is not exclusive of others. The afterlife theory held by some is that there is nothing existing past physical death, that we become nothing more than worm food. The end of life, like slapping a mosquito, is squashed forever. To believe that death is the absolute end would render the spiritual realm nonexistent. The apparition taught me that there is another realm of life that exists unseen by human eyes. Unseen, unless we are allowed a peek into that other world.

Experiencing the appearance of the apparition left me feeling much like the blind man recorded in the New Testament of the Bible.

[17] So they said again to the blind man, "What do you say about him, since he has opened your eyes?" He said, "He is a prophet." [18] The Jews did not believe that he had been blind and had received his sight, until they called the parents of the man who had received his sight [19] and asked them, "Is this your son, who you say was born blind? How then does he now see?" [20] His parents answered, "We

know that this is our son and that he was born blind.[21] But how he now sees we do not know, nor do we know who opened his eyes. Ask him; he is of age. He will speak for himself."[22] (His parents said these things because they feared the Jews, for the Jews had already agreed that if anyone should confess Jesus to be Christ, he was to be put out of the synagogue.) [23] Therefore, his parents said, "He is of age; ask him." [24] So, for the second time they called the man who had been blind and said to him, "Give glory to God. We know that this man is a sinner." [25] He answered, "Whether he is a sinner I do not know. One thing I do know, that though I was blind, now I see" (John 9.17-25).

The blind man had been blind since birth, people in town knew of his blindness. What is truly astounding is that he was healed miraculously, without any medical procedure, in a time and culture where being blind was a forever condition. No medical treatments available, no hope of ever gaining sight. The blind man really knew nothing about Jesus, and when questioned by the local leaders he only expressed one undeniable fact. He was blind and now he is not. He was certain of that one thing. He could now see. How? Why? He did not know. Why was he singled out and healed? He was not one of high standing in the community; he sat in public daily and begged. He was considered a nobody that people walked by daily, without giving him a thought, and if they did, it was to give him some coins to help him survive.

He was given the gift of sight, not earning the gift, certainly not deserving the gift any more than the hundreds of others who were blind. Why him? What set him apart? What is so special about this one blind man? Nothing really. He is singled out for no apparent reason. "One thing I do know, that though I was blind, now I see." This is all he knows, he now sees. Something supernatural has occurred, and the blind man is no longer blind.

Belief in the accuracy of the events in the Bible is important to be able to answer the possibility of supernatural events. In this story, the only question needing an answer is whether it is possible that supernatural, miraculous events do occur, and then if so, why do they occur? What is the purpose, for what reason? Magicians can perform tricks that defy explanation, yet we see the trick performed. Is seeing believing? Go back to the purpose. What is the purpose of the trick? Possibly for entertainment, to fill the arena with paying ticket holders so the magician can earn a living. We laugh and applaud, enjoying the magic tricks, even though we do not understand how the trick is performed. We see the trick, the sleight of hand. Even though our understanding cannot comprehend the "how," we do know the "why." The magician needs to earn a living.

We can see something without understanding, but it in no way nullifies the thing seen. Something appearing to be very much real and authentic occasionally leaves us with no understanding of how or why it appears.

For myself, like the blind man in the Biblical example, the purpose of the event may be to create a change in the person witnessing the event. In the case of the blind man, he now sees. Something supernatural has happened to him. In my case, I now know the spiritual realm is very real. This has created a huge change in the way I view almost everything. Like the man born blind who now sees, I have seen as well. An encounter with the spiritual realm changed everything. I now know, looking back for more than forty years, just how much the impact of the visual sight of the spiritual realm has affected me.

CHAPTER 35

Burnout

I distinctly remember thinking during my first shifts as a paramedic that if this job ever seemed routine or normal to me, there would be something wrong with my perception of things. A person can't smell a sewer if exposed to the smell long enough. I feared that this job would permanently, negatively affect me.

In some ways it did. I have witnessed many veteran paramedics burn out over the years. One of my paramedic friends who worked at a working firehouse, not one of my partners, but a veteran paramedic, experienced burnout. The patient was complaining of hand pain and wanted the paramedic to take him to the hospital by ambulance. Tired and frustrated, the paramedic walked the patient over in front of the ambulance and turned the headlights on the high-beam setting. He placed the patient's hand on the surface of the headlight, looked at the hand on the headlight much like an x-ray machine then told the patient in a condescending voice, "You can see that none of the bones are broken; you don't need an ambulance," and refused transport to the patient. This is a classic case of an otherwise excellent paramedic experiencing burnout.

The job takes a toll, and typically the one burned out is the last one to know they are burned out. The saving grace of burnout is that the one experiencing it does not have to stay that way. A nice long vacation, psychological therapy, and discussions with other paramedics all help the one who has gone into mental overload.

It happened to me. I burned out. I didn't know it, but my partner noticed it. It happened when we received a call for a shooting in the projects. We arrived on scene and found a young man outside the apartment suffering from a gunshot wound. My partner rendered medical aid to the man while I went into the apartment to check for more victims. Inside the apartment, was a woman with two stab wounds to the abdomen but conscious. In the 1980s it was acceptable to take two critically wounded patients to the hospital in the same ambulance due to the lack of resources. One paramedic would drive, the other would render care to both victims in the back of the ambulance en route to the hospital. My partner and I loaded both patients. Before jumping in the driver's seat to drive us to the hospital, my partner asked me how bad her injuries were. I replied, "She's ok. She just has two stab wounds to the gut."

In my mind, I was trying to relay to my partner that she would probably survive, that her vital signs were fairly stable at that moment, but the words I used clearly expressed my burn out. On the way back to the firehouse after unloading the patients at the hospital, my partner called me out on my choice of words to describe the female patient's condition. My partner rightly recognized my burn out, of which I was totally unaware. After my shift was over, I drove home and went to sleep.

When I woke up my wife and I went to a birthday party where one of our children got hurt while playing. It was a scraped knee, but my son was visibly upset and crying. I said that he would be fine and went about whatever I was doing. My wife became irate because of my lack of attention to our son and told me that unless the kids' guts are hanging out, I don't even notice their injuries. She was right,

I had mentally arrived at the burn-out stage, where medical care was robotic and without compassion.

I hated who I was becoming. The job was changing me, and not in a positive way. I knew I had to cut back on my constant exposure to trauma and suffering. I needed a long vacation. I needed to refuse to work overtime for a while.

It was hard, both emotionally, knowing who I was becoming and not liking it one damn bit, and financially, needing to cut back on purchases to keep the budget balanced without the benefit of overtime pay. So many triggers daily. The smell of antifreeze or battery acid would trigger gruesome vehicle accidents I had witnessed and worked. Shopping in some department stores would be a trigger because the sound of the tone used to alert customer service in certain department stores sounded just like the sound used by the fire department to signal another emergency call.

Compartmentalizing my work life and my home life in separate parts of my brain created a dual personality that would manifest in nightmares and night sweats. Adrenalin drain at work would leave nothing in the tank when off duty. Off-duty time was spent recuperating from the job instead of being lived out to the fullest relationally with family and friends. There had to be more to life than this. I felt like I was sliding into the abyss, fighting and clawing against the descent. I needed meaning, structure, and balance to supplant near constant chaos. Knowing, in the far reaches of my brain, that there was more to this life than what I was experiencing helped me to gradually turn the corner toward recovery. It was slow, but curative. Seeing the apparition has helped me to focus more on what awaits me and others in the spiritual realm, instead of the constant bombardment of daily pressure in the present.

CHAPTER 36

Take Pills, Wash Them
Down With Bleach

L ife in the projects without the means to support one's self and
with dim prospects for anything good in life usually results in
one of two paths. One group will seek relief from the pain in the
form of drug or alcohol abuse. This large group kept firefighters and
paramedics busy most shifts. The other group, a much smaller
group in my observation, would keep striving to find ways to have a
better life if possible.

It was after midnight. The call came in as a toxic ingestion,
which is the politically correct term for overdose. The call was in a
construction zone, which is unusual for an overdose. We arrived on
scene to find a very large, muscular young man had broken into a
construction trailer and eaten everything in the medicine cabinet.
He was distraught, wanting to die, but not symptomatic yet. We
talked him off the ledge enough to get him to agree to go to the hospital with us, so he walked to the ambulance and sat on the stretcher.

Not wanting to do battle with Goliath, we continually tried to
reduce his anxiety. He rode on the stretcher, restrained by the chest
and leg seat belts, as I sat in the captain's chair next to him. We got

on the interstate and approached highway speed. About five minutes from the hospital, he unbuckled his seat belts and lunged for the back door of the ambulance. I tried to stop him, but he elbowed me back out of his way, while at the same time, throwing open the back doors. We were doing about sixty miles per hour when he climbed out onto the rear bumper. When he opened the back doors, it set off a warning light in the cab. My partner immediately started braking hard which caused the patient not to be able to jump because of the rapid deceleration force. When he finally was able to jump off the back bumper, the ambulance was barely rolling, so he fell on his face in the middle of the interstate.

In an attempt to restrain him, my partner jumped on the patient's back while he was still lying on the pavement. I climbed out of the ambulance and sat on the patient's back as he tried bucking us off like a bull in a rodeo arena. This whole scene was rapidly devolving into the gray area, as neither one of us really knew what to do about this situation. We couldn't let him up, he was now a danger to everyone including himself. We couldn't keep him down; he was already proving too strong for the both of us to handle. We were already past the eight seconds required for a successful bull ride with still no help in sight. If we stayed in the middle of the interstate much longer, we wouldn't have to worry about either scenario as we would all be run over and killed by traffic.

Suddenly a car screeched to a halt right next to us. There were three young men in the car offering to help us. The five of us got the patient reloaded in the ambulance and tied his arms and legs to a backboard on the stretcher, cinching the cravats securely so as not to have a repeat performance of his former escape attempt.

Arriving at the hospital, we wheeled him in while he was fully restrained on the stretcher. The receiving nurse told us to put him in a room. The doctor came in with two more nurses, they all wanted to know why such a gentle young man was restrained like a combative criminal. We told our version of the events leading up to getting him to the hospital, and they all looked at the patient's sweet, gentle- giant face with no words coming from his mouth.

Immediately, they started to untie him. My partner and I both warned the receiving medical staff of the dangers of untying him. Before they could get one arm loose, he flexed his muscles and broke the other remaining restraints, at which time they all started screaming for security. We loaded our stretcher and got back in service for the next emergency.

We continued to get calls for toxic ingestions every shift. Less than two weeks after the call where the man jumped out on the interstate, we received a call for another overdose that tried to jump out of the ambulance onto the interstate. This patient also wanted to kill himself, so he decided drinking bleach would be a good idea. After loading him in the ambulance we got on the interstate and approached highway speed. He took his seat belts loose from the stretcher and opened the back doors of the ambulance. He climbed out on the rear bumper but couldn't jump because I was able to grab him and hold him from behind by his belt, while holding a grab bar on the ceiling of the ambulance with my other hand to keep me from being pulled out with him. My partner got the ambulance stopped and helped me pull him back into the ambulance and secure him. We continued to the hospital without further incident.

What makes perfectly healthy people want to kill themselves? I had no idea there were so many attempted suicides until I started working in my job. It's not unusual to respond to at least one attempted suicide per shift. Some are very successful at killing themselves, others seem to be trying to get someone's attention. Self-inflicted gunshot wounds, hangings, and carbon monoxide poisonings seem to be the most successful methods of ending one's life, while cutting wrists, taking pills, or threats of suicide are sometimes, but not always, cries for help by someone not serious about dying.

To attempt suicide at all, the person must get to a place where life is too painful, physically and or mentally, to want to continue living. Some people are too afraid to end their lives, so they arm themselves and commit a crime to get a police officer to shoot them. Suicide by cop. The result is the same.

Anxiety and depression can be precursors to attempted suicide, but not always. Sometimes there are no signs. A paramedic I knew well hung himself. We worked together at the same firehouse. I had interacted with him the shift before he killed himself and he showed no sign of anything being wrong. He had obviously reached a state of mind that anything must be better than his life, so he rolled the dice on an afterlife, choosing the uncertainty of life after death over the gnawing pain of his current life. Imagining how bad it must get for a person to intentionally cut their life short was beyond what I could fathom. Conversely, there are others living lives of near unbearable pain and misery every day with no thought of suicide. I'm still not sure what triggers a person to make the decision to end it all. I hope I never get to that place.

All I know is that there are far too many people out there who are barely hanging onto the ragged edge of life. For me, having witnessed the reality of a spiritual realm, I know for certain there is more to life than our physical reality. I've seen it.

CHAPTER 37

The Risk of Having Money

Living in poverty with the crumbs of life can lead a person to commit crimes they would never think about doing if there were just a little relief from their constant need. However, poverty does not affect all poor people the same. In the projects, one apartment might be a shooting gallery with all types of drug abuse and prostitution-full of trash, filth, and crime. Next door might live a family or individuals that don't play that game. Their apartment is spotless. Their hygiene is good. They dress clean and nice but still live in poverty. The difference between the two types of tenants must be internal, a mode of being that transcends outward circumstances. These types of people are the ones you see on the news after suffering the loss of everything material in a tornado or flood, calmly saying that they are glad to just be alive and that they will start with nothing and rebuild. Sadly, many people living in poverty choose crime instead.

It was 1:00 am on a hot summer night. The call came in as a traffic accident in the neighborhood. We arrived at the location and found a taxi on a dark residential street with no one outside. Even at 1:00 am it was very strange to arrive on scene and find nobody around. The car's front fender was touching a tree, with no apparent damage to either the car or tree. Everything was eerily quiet. Normally, on a hot summer night, bystanders would be everywhere around the scene. People would be pointing out the wreck as children rode their bicycles around the vehicle. The driver of the taxi was sitting in the driver's seat, unconscious, but breathing. His breathing was labored, and he was sweating profusely. There was no visual evidence of anything being wrong with the driver, but his vital signs were weak, like someone who had suffered a serious traumatic injury associated with hypovolemia, a blood volume loss.

His skin, shirt, pants, and shoes were all black. We put him in the ambulance and treated him for hypovolemic shock en route to the hospital, still with no outward sign of injury. At the hospital, we gave our report to the receiving doc, with the explanation that we didn't know what was wrong with him. We were just treating him based on his symptoms and our findings. The trauma surgeons called us in later and showed us the cause of the injury. They held his black shirt up to a bright light and we could now see a small pin hole in the shirt in what would be the chest area if he were wearing it. The surgeons told us he had likely been ice picked in the chest, possibly an attempted robbery. He was seriously injured but survived.

It was now 2:30 am and another call came in for a shooting. This call was on the edge of the downtown area, in a dark alley. The shooting victim was a small Hispanic lady, middle aged and well dressed. She owned a nearby bar and was in the process of closing the bar for the night and taking the earnings from the evening sales with her in a little bag when she was shot.

The shooter shot her for the money bag, which he took from her. She was equally upset about the robbery and being shot. We put her in the ambulance and began our head-to-toe assessment. She was bleeding from the left hip area, but not heavily. In order to assess her injuries, we removed her pants and had to cut her underwear off. In the process of cutting off the underwear, a large caliber bullet fell onto the floor of the ambulance. It appeared to be a .45 caliber, which had entered her left buttocks, went through the buttocks, and exited on the hip side lodging in her underwear. It made no sense why a large-caliber bullet would not have gone clean through the clothing and continued on, but for some reason it didn't. I was holding the bullet in my hand. We transported her to the hospital.

I was cleaning the back of the ambulance and restocking supplies, pondering why crimes like these–the ice-picked man and the lady with the gunshot wound–happened so often, but they do. Both patients survived, but near-death experiences can change us all. The realization of the transience of life, after having life nearly cut short, can create a different person in all of us. The wow-that-was- close phenomenon can affect more than just firefighters.

CHAPTER 38

A Gun Doesn't Guarantee Victory

It was around noon on a warm afternoon. I was at work, sitting at the kitchen table of the firehouse with other firefighters. The bay doors were open to the street, so it was easy to hear what was going on outside. Suddenly we heard loud voices from men yelling at each other. We ran outside to find three men. One was lying in the street next to the curb while another man kicked him in the head. His bloody head repeatedly recoiled from the kicker's boot to the curb and back to the boot. His head was a bloody mess. The kicker had a pistol in his hand but was not using it. The other man stood and watched everything in silence.

My paramedic partner talked the kicker into giving him the gun as we tried to defuse the situation. It turned out that the gun belonged to the man who was getting his head kicked in and who was now unconscious. It seemed the kicker managed to take the gun away from the shooter after the shooter shot the kicker's brother, who was the silent bystander. I asked the silent bystander if he had been shot and he said, "Yes." He pointed to a bullet hole in his shirt, in the middle of his chest area. We took the man who had been shot in the chest, still asymptomatic, to the hospital. He had a very small amount of blood on his skin where he said the bullet entered. His vital signs were normal. He acted as if he had a mosquito bite instead of a gunshot wound to the chest. At the hospital, his chest x-ray revealed that he had indeed been shot in the chest, in the center of his sternum bone in the middle of his chest. The small-caliber bullet was still lodged in the bone of his sternum. The bullet broke the skin on his chest and immediately lodged in the bone, causing no damage other than a small hole. Had the bullet entered his body a half an inch to the right or left it would have gone right into his heart, possibly causing a fatal injury.

You never know how a story ends, until it does. In this case, the shooter should have had the upper hand but ended up with the most serious injuries. The one brother, the kicker, should have been at a terrible disadvantage facing a gunman, but gained the upper hand. Lastly, the gunshot victim ended up being the luckiest man in the world.

Cognitively processing this emergency leaves one with only a feeling of the fragility of life–in this case, a difference of a half an inch from where the bullet struck his chest. Everyone dies. Knowing this, it begs the question: Is there more to life than what we know as life? The answer from my perspective is a resounding, "Yes!" I've seen another realm that is just as real.

CHAPTER 39

Say No to PCP

It was cold. Cold enough to wear a jacket. After midnight the call came in as an unknown. We rolled to the end of a dead-end, dark street in the neighborhood. At the end of the street there was a lone police car with the policeman standing outside his vehicle patiently waiting for us. He was alone, there was no one else around–only stillness, with an occasional sound piercing the silence with what sounded like a large animal growling and snarling in a loud, eerie, unnerving manner. The policeman shined his flashlight toward the eerie noise. The noise was coming from a large drainage ditch past the dead end of the street. Pinpointing his flashlight beam on a large brush pile in the center of the ditch, the officer said that he thought the noise originated from the brush pile. The brush pile appeared to be about twelve feet tall; likely illegally dumped by local tree trimmers to avoid paying dump fees. It consisted of cut branches, thorn bushes, and miscellaneous vegetation. The brush pile was about thirty yards from the end of the dead-end street where we were standing.

I asked the officer what the sound was. He said he did not know but said that he waited for us to get on scene because he did not want to go down there by himself. I get it, the sound was beyond creepy. No moon and overcast skies made it appear unusually dark, a darkness with which structure firefighters are familiar. Crawling through heavy black smoke in a burning structure trying to locate the fire is at times a total blackness. Experienced firefighters searching for the main body of fire in a structure learn to guide themselves with their ears. If their right ear is hotter than their left, they crawl toward the right. If the left ear is hotter, they crawl toward the left.

The three of us started walking down into the drainage culvert. The total darkness made our footing sketchy while we walked over uneven, overgrown terrain following the cop's nervously shaking flashlight beam that danced over every possible threat. We all followed the flashlight beam as the growling and snarling became louder as we approached the brush pile. Standing, staring at the brush pile, the three of us tried to follow the flashlight beam.

There appeared to be nothing visible other than a massive pile of brush, with the snarling sound emanating from somewhere inside the brush pile. The cop stood a few feet from the brush pile holding the flashlight as still as possible while my partner and I clumsily scaled the pile of brush trying to get on top of it. Limbs crunched beneath our feet as we finally scaled to the top of the pile and started removing branches one by one, throwing them off the pile as best we could. The snarling from below our feet, coupled with the lack of light from the angle of the cop's flashlight beam shining from his position on the ground, was beginning to cause an uneasy feeling in me. I hated not being able to see, especially with a potential danger lurking under my feet that was snarling like a badger with its paw caught in a trap.

After we removed the top five feet of branches we could see where the sound was coming from. Lying on his back in the middle of the brush pile was a young man, maybe eighteen to twenty years old. He was growling louder than ever now that he sensed our presence and continued to thrash around in the brush.

No audible words came from his mouth, only wild-animal noises. Angry noises, mixed with desperation and dread. He was wearing a white shirt. The t-shirt was shredded from the thorny branches, with blood from the hundreds of scratches on his torso staining what remained of the t-shirt. He was wearing tight blue jeans soaked with urine, with lacerated, bloody, bare feet protruding from the jeans. His face and neck were covered in bloody scratches from the thorny bushes, and foamy saliva covered his cheeks and chin. He had orange hair on his face and head, and white, mottled, bloody, freckled skin soaked with sweat. Green, bloodshot, glassy eyes peered out from the brush. He appeared to be getting progressively more agitated now that he knew we were there. His intense animal eyes focused on us like a predator focusing on his prey–ready to attack, kill, and eat.

The police officer had a handful of plastic zip-tie restraints in his trembling hands. The improvised plan, operationally falling well into the gray area, was to get him off the brush pile and restrain him so we could load him in the ambulance. I tried to grab the bottom of his blue jeans and pull him out of the middle of the brush pile. He recoiled and I lost my grip. I tried again and got a better grip and started to move him. At this point he flexed his body like he was doing a sit up and lunged at my hand pulling on his pants leg. Instead of grabbing my hand with his hands and prying my hand loose, he snapped at me like an animal trying to bite me. His bizarre behavior, trying to bite when both his hands were free, made me immediately aware of his extreme level of altered reality. I let go of his pants, having narrowly escaped his snapping teeth.

His reality was so altered that he would not remember anything later, like a drunk driver who runs over and kills pedestrians and wakes up the next day in jail, not knowing what had happened. After we repeated the process of trying to grab his pants leg without losing a finger, we finally got him off the brush pile. The officer used plastic zip ties on his wrists and legs, then we loaded him on a scoop stretcher and tied him tightly to the stretcher. We carried the scoop stretcher with him on board, growling and snarling the whole way up to the ambulance. I got in the back of the ambulance with him as we transported him to the hospital. He continued to thrash around, foaming, spitting and growling all the way to the hospital. His green, bloodshot eyes were continually fixed on me, with his neck veins bulging and protruding. It occurred to me that his behavior was like that of the demoniac described in the scriptures. I do not know much about demons, other than what I've read in the scriptures, but based on the information described in the scriptures, I would say this scene bore an eerie resemblance.

Due to the combative nature of the patient and my desire not to get bitten, we arrived at the hospital without a patient assessment report. After briefing the receiving staff, we were back in service. The receiving nurses speculated that the patient may have ingested PCP, but nothing definite yet. I'm just glad we got the green-eyed, bloody, urine soaked, frothing, spitting, snarling, orange, predator man out of our ambulance.

CHAPTER 40

Life Without Friends

It was a cold, Christmas-season evening. We made it back to the firehouse and were looking forward to a little downtime when a call came in for chest pains. We arrived at the house, a middle-class home in a settled neighborhood. No little kids around in this neighborhood, mostly older folks with grown children, many being reluctant empty nesters. A fake-blonde, short-haired, mid-fifties woman answered the door. She was very polite, telling us to come on in and have a seat, like she had invited us for tea. We were expecting someone with a heart attack or serious chest pains, so we asked where the patient was. She said she was the only one in the house and that she lived alone. She said she called because she had chest pains. Not appearing in any distress, we began with a patient assessment and a lengthy questionnaire about her medical history and present pain.

Not long into the assessment, my partner suspected she was formulating a fictitious medical condition. He asked her if she had family, and if so, where were they. She replied that she has one family member, a grown son, who lived two thousand miles away. Apparently, he never contacted his mother. Sadness fell on her countenance while telling the story; we sat and listened. She was obviously not having a medical emergency.

She admitted that she didn't have any chest pain, or any other pain for that matter, but called 911 to get someone to come to her house so that she would have someone to talk to. Right before Christmas, spending the holiday season alone was too much for her to bear. She broke down crying and asked if we could stay longer, just to talk to her. We told her that we really couldn't, we needed to get back in service for another call in case there was another emergency in our response district. She put her hands on both of our arms and looked us in the eyes, with the heaviest sadness in hers, as she said she would give us each a thousand dollars if we would just stay for a little while. The desperation in her voice made me hurt inside, because I knew the answer had to be no. We gathered up our gear and quietly left after refusing her offer. No words of "Merry Christmas" seemed appropriate. Her Christmas was far from merry.

Back in the ambulance, I began thinking about the different types of pain. Of course, everyone is familiar with physical pain and how devastating it can be, but her emotional pain seemed equally as scarring.

I learned something that evening that I still carry with me. Even though my training as a paramedic encompassed medical emergencies, we, all of us, are part of the human race. When someone else is hurting, it is okay to empathize with the emotional pain–it keeps us human. The difficulty arises in trying to meter the empathy extended to others and still be able to perform emergency work without also becoming a patient.

EPILOGUE

Going Forward...Changed Forever

God seeks you out to play a role in His story.
God makes a way for you to engage in His story.
God has forgiven your darkest sin.
God can use you regardless of your past.
God doesn't want to leave you out.

I realize I am on a journey, this path we call life, with all the random dynamics that come into play. *What does it all mean? What else can be said?* I am older by worldly standards. Life, and all it entails with the struggles, suffering, joy, and elation is winding down for me. I still strive for the meta goal: to grow spiritually closer to God, to know Him more fully in this life. I understand nothing in relation to all there is. I am in creation seeking the One outside creation, Elohim, "Creator God." He has given me a glimpse of a world that is metaphysically real, existing alongside the physical world–the only realm I have known, until the apparition.

Post apparition, knowing that there is another world outside of the one we know and experience daily, I find that I view everything, especially God, in a different way. This realization has altered the way I process life, whether it be secular or spiritual. As far as my job is concerned, I worked thirty-five years in the fire department as a firefighter and emergency medical worker. In retrospect, the apparition enabled me to process events while doing this job with the overriding clarity and knowledge that everything in life is always more than it seems, from the smallest tasks to the biggest challenges, because it all fits into a world beyond the world that we perceive in the physical realm. With the new realization that God sees me, it changed how I perceive God. El Roi, in Hebrew, means "the God who sees." All my personal actions, hidden thoughts and feelings, whereabouts, and plans are known by God, seen by God, even before they transpire. I am comforted by this new revelation. The comfort comes even though God knows my inner thoughts and desires, my goals and aspirations, my sin and shortcomings. Everything about me is laid bare before His omniscient eye. Comfort comes because there is nothing standing in the way of Him knowing me fully and completely. I am naked in the garden, like Adam and Eve. Whatever I've done, God already knows. Whatever I'm preparing to do, God already knows. There is something very honest and truthful about a relationship such as this, therein lies comfort. Nothing is hidden. He is the great "I Am," recorded in Exodus, and I am nothing. He is the One who showed me the apparition, clear and precise, timely, complete, life-changing, and enough. Like the bridge that connected those hurting and in need in our fire district to their rescuers, the apparition became a bridge connecting my emotionally inadequate state to a life lived with a supernatural safety net supporting my emotional health as I cognitively attempted to process all the "Wow, that was close!" that I would experience going forward. This "bridge" was enough to permanently span the course of my life. Enough to allow me to gaze deeply into the darkness that this life can bring and to keep fighting. Enough to ground me in hope in the midst of suffering. Enough to dispel the notion that this physical life is all there is. Enough to bring me to my knees in prayer when life challenged me beyond my perceived limitations. Enough to make me humble, with a heart of thankfulness toward a gracious, merciful, omnipotent God. Thank you, Lord.

WORKS CITED

English Standard Version. Bible Gateway, https://www.biblegateway.com, Accessed 15 December 2023.

"Jonestown." *FBI Records: The Vault,* Federal Bureau of Investigations, https://vault.fbi.gov/jonestown, Accessed 8 December 2023.

Peterson, Jordan. *Beyond Order: 12 More Rules for Life.* Penguin-Portfolio, 2021.

Solzhenitsyn, Alexandr. *The Gulag Archipelago.* The Harvill Press. 2003.